Looking Back, Moving Forward

THE SOUTHWEST GEORGIA FREEDOM STRUGGLE

1814-2014

BY LEE W. FORMWALT

For Georgia Schaich, fellow traveller, with love + best wishes, Lee Formwalt

SPONSORS

PHOEBE PUTNEY MEMORIAL HOSPITAL | HERITAGEBANK OF THE SOUTH

MILLERCOORS | JANE WILLSON

Albany Civil Rights Institute   Georgia Humanities Council

2014

Published by the Albany Civil Rights Institute and the Georgia Humanities Council

326 Whitney Ave, P.O. Box 6036   50 Hurt Plaza, S.E., Suite 595

Albany, GA 31706-6036   Atlanta, GA 30303

(229) 432-1698   (404) 523-6220

www.albanycivilrightsinstitute.org   www.georgiahumanities.org

ISBN   978-0-692-21940-9

By Lee W. Formwalt, Ph.D.

Designed by Cathy Cowdrey

Photography by A. Radclyffe Dugmore, Benjamin F. Cochran, Danny Lyon, and Todd Stone

Printed in the U.S.A.

The proceeds from the sale of this book will benefit the Albany Civil Rights Institute.
Additional copies of *Looking Back, Moving Forward* may be ordered from
ACRI, P.O. Box 6036, Albany, GA 31706-6036.

Cover: Photograph of the water fountains in the Dougherty County Courthouse, Albany, made by
Danny Lyon, August 1962. See Chapter 8. Danny Lyon/Magnum Photos

Foreword

For me, an important thread in the worldwide narrative of human and civil rights is the story told in this book. It is a story—or more properly, stories—masterfully told, involving a place upon whose ground we stand. What I most admire is the book's authoritative approach, straightforward and feelingly conveyed. Drawing from published and unpublished sources and the product of a career of scholarship, service, and leadership, this book is a gift of discovery and remembrance.

Almost 400 years ago, traders brought Africans to the first English colony in the New World, Virginia, where tobacco plantations and slavery grew hand in hand, and spread. Four of the young nation's first five presidents, Virginians, owned slaves, even as they trumpeted the universal values of liberty and constitution.

In the first half of the 19th century, owing to the ingenuity of Eli Whitney and his cotton gin, the cotton economy quickly established itself in the southern states, spreading rapidly west below the Mason Dixon line into Texas, and as far north as Missouri. Deep in that South was Georgia, and in the southwest corner of the state, cotton plantations sprang up that relied on the forced labor of an entire population. Albany became the economic and transportation hub of the region, and would remain so into the twenty-first century.

Though limited to the South (at least legally) after 1804, American slavery was an economic dynamo that demanded more and more land to meet expanding demands for the fiber in New England's and Europe's mills. As a land-hungry South faced an increasingly abolitionist North (or at least a North whose majority found the institution of slavery repugnant), the country broke apart in civil war over the question of slavery's future within the established boundaries of the United States. The South's objective in seceding was to evade the dictates of Congress (and the new president, Abraham Lincoln) by creating its own national republic for white people, one dedicated to the protection and perpetuation of human bondage.

Though the South was not to succeed in this vision, there remained those who enforced another kind of slavery as manifested in the Jim Crow laws. Over 250 years of slavery transitioned to a segregation policy that continued to thwart and distort the lives of millions of American citizens who lived under these laws. Were it not for freedom movements, like the one in Albany, racism in its more virulent form would still be flourishing in parts of this country. Watersheds in freedom movements present opportunities to keep our country moving toward the Declaration of Independence mandate: a free society based on true equality. This is hardly a single generation's work. It is a society's ongoing work. And what Albany did was nothing less than establish another watershed for freedom and human rights movements, one that emerged in a spectacular and selfless way, emphasizing brotherhood, peace, and freedom.

The Albany Movement is a testimonial to the human spirit and the possibilities of growth and social change. Albany indeed is a herald, in my view, one whose remembrance is a necessity in the long road of freedom struggles everywhere. There is still so much to be done in the United States. And there is so much to be done in our world. This narrative honors those who have played a part in this important work and invites us to play ours.

Jamil Zainaldin, President
Georgia Humanities Council

Preface

Looking Back, Moving Forward: The Southwest Georgia Freedom Struggle, 1814-2014 is a publication of the Albany Civil Rights Institute (ACRI) and the Georgia Humanities Council. ACRI had its beginnings in the Old Mt. Zion Baptist Church at the corner of Whitney Avenue and Jefferson Street in Albany, Georgia. Old Mt. Zion and Shiloh Baptist Church, right across the street from each other, were the sites of numerous mass meetings during the heyday of the early 1960s civil rights movement in Albany, county seat of Dougherty County, in the heart of southwest Georgia. After the Mt. Zion congregation moved to a new location, a group of community leaders in the early 1990s organized a nonprofit corporation to establish a civil rights museum. The Mt. Zion congregation donated the old church to the nonprofit organization and the building was placed on the National Register of Historic Places.

of the larger national civil rights movement which many people consider to have begun either in 1954 with the *Brown v. Board of Education* Supreme Court decision declaring public school segregation unconstitutional, or in 1955 with the Montgomery Bus Boycott when the young minister Dr. Martin Luther King, Jr. emerged as a civil rights leader of national renown. The movement is often considered to have concluded either in 1964-1965 with the passage of the Civil Rights and Voting Rights acts, or in 1968 with the assassination of Martin Luther King, Jr. in Memphis, Tennessee.

Many historians are rethinking the chronological boundaries of the movement which make it a 1950s and 1960s phenomenon. Instead, they propose what they call the Long Civil Rights Movement which began before 1954 and did not end in 1968, but continues right up to the

Key players in igniting the Albany Movement were Charles Sherrod and the Student Nonviolent Coordinating Committee (SNCC). Martin Luther King, Jr. came in 1961 and left in 1962, but Sherrod and SNCC stayed.

In addition to deeding the old church to the corporation, Mt. Zion members donated $25,000 for the creation of the Albany Civil Rights Movement Museum. Dougherty County provided $750,000 for the project; the city of Albany gave $250,000; and the museum board raised an additional $100,000 from private individuals and businesses. The $1.2 million renovation was completed in 1998 and the museum opened on the 37th anniversary of the founding of the Albany Movement in November 1961. The museum founders' dream for a new building with separate exhibit space next to the church was realized in October 2008, when the $4 million facility was dedicated as the new Albany Civil Rights Institute.

The Albany Civil Rights Institute is devoted to telling the story of the Albany and Southwest Georgia Movement. For some people that means the years 1961-1962 when Martin Luther King, Jr. came to town and participated in the movement. The Albany Movement came to be part

present. In the Long Civil Rights Movement we look to those earlier and later attempts by African Americans and others to assert their human and civil rights.

Some would argue that the civil rights movement began in the 1930s; others go back to the beginning of the 20th century when the NAACP was founded. Still others go back to emancipation and Reconstruction in the 19th century. Others argue that the movement began with slavery and those enslaved persons who resisted their bondage. In other words, most historians agree that the freedom struggle for civil rights was not limited to two decades in the middle 20th century, but has a long history that goes back to before our nation's founding and continues right up through today.

This book tells the story of the Long Southwest Georgia Movement, going all the way back to the earliest white and African American settlers in southwest Georgia. Greed and white privilege on the one hand, and resistance and a yearning for freedom and equality on the other have been continual themes in southwest Georgia history in the last two centuries. Quickly summarized, the story of its early years consists of the white man defeating the red man in the Creek War, 1813-1814, and taking his land to grow the white gold of that day—cotton. To clear the land, and to plant and cultivate the crop, he brought in the enslaved black man, and laid what W.E.B. Du Bois called "the corner-stone of the Cotton Kingdom." That kingdom, built on African American slavery, came crashing down

white northerners and southerners reconciled as the 19th century ended, ushering in the long dark years of Jim Crow, and segregation became the law of the land south of the Mason Dixon line. White supremacy was reinforced by law and by extralegal violence, the worst of which was lynching. As during slavery and Reconstruction, African Americans resisted the system of oppression. Some left southwest Georgia; others organized and laid the ground-work for the Albany civil rights movement which burst on the national scene in late 1961. The eyes of the nation and

SNCC workers Randy Battle and Charles Sherrod canvass for voter registration in southwest Georgia. Danny Lyon/Magnum Photos

with emancipation at the conclusion of the Civil War in 1865. There followed in the brief hopeful years of Reconstruction in southwest Georgia (1865-1871) a struggle to make African American freedom real. With the spotty protection of the federal government, black men by the hundreds elected African American men to represent them in the state legislature. They built their own churches, schools, and social institutions.

Federal support of the experiment in African American freedom did not last long. The bonds of race were strong;

the world were on southwest Georgia and witnessed the largest direct action community protest at that time in American history.

Key players in igniting the Albany Movement were Charles Sherrod and the Student Nonviolent Coordinating Committee (SNCC). Martin Luther King, Jr. came in 1961 and left in 1962, but Sherrod and SNCC stayed. Their stories flesh out the narrative of the southwest Georgia movement in the 1960s. Once again the federal government allied itself with the African American liberation cause, but

Preface (cont.)

it was local people of color who went to court and, in county after county in the region, brought the white power structure kicking and screaming into the modern world of equal rights and diversity. The struggle for freedom and equality continues in the 21st century as whites continue to avoid true public school integration and wield economic power in their own interest. One thing that continues to inspire contemporary freedom fighters is the story of how their predecessors challenged oppression. We, at the Albany Civil Rights Institute, are pleased to share that epic tale with you.

A work of history like this rests on both primary sources and the work of other historians and writers who have labored in the fields of southwest Georgia and civil rights history, especially Susan Eva O'Donovan, David Williams, Eric Foner, Leon F. Litwack, W.E.B. Du Bois, Mary G. Rolinson, Fitzhugh Brundage, Hugh Pearson, Aaron Brown, B. Carlyle Ramsey, Stephen G.N. Tuck, Michael Chalfen, Taylor Branch, David J. Garrow, Raymond Arsenault, Andrew Young, William G. Anderson, Guy and Candie Carawan, Mary Royal Jenkins, Clayborne Carson, Jason Sokol, Pat Watters, John Perdew, Howard Zinn, David L. Chappell, Emilye Crosby, Todd Moye, Alisa Y. Harrison, Janie Culbreth Rambeau, Annette Jones White, Bernice Johnson Reagon, Joann Christian Mants, McCree L. Harris, Rutha Mae Harris, Carolyn Daniels, Peggy Trotter Dammond Preacely, Prathia Hall, Faith S. Holsaert, Racquel Henry, Casey Hayden, Joan Browning, Dorothea Irwin, Penny Patch, Jack Chatfield, Peter de Lissovoy, Dennis Roberts, Randy Battle, Charles and Shirley Sherrod, Pete Seeger, Bobby Burch, Carolynn Segers, James B. Wall, John E. Moore, Tracy Elaine K'Meyer, John Cole Vodicka, Mary Jo Haywood, Alma Noble, Betty Williams, James Griffin, Irene Turner, Helen Young, Herbert and Connie Phipps, Tom Seegmueller, Hasan Kwame Jeffries, Stephanie J. Shaw, Joseph Kitchens, John Inscoe, Titus Brown, Jeffrey Kolnick, David Dennard, Patricia Sullivan, Christopher Waldrep, Michael Fitzgerald, Wilma King, Angela Whitmal, Parris Larrain, Damon Freeman, William Chafe, Darlene Clarke Hine, James O. Horton, John Dittmer, David Blight, Constance Curry, Robin D.G. Kelley, John D'Emilio, Renee Romano, Danielle McGuire, Waldo Martin, Peniel Joseph, Penne Laubenthal, Leslie McLemore, Susan Bagby, Michelle Deardorff, Rose Gladney, Marge Harris, Tim Huebner, Shirley Jackson, Charles McDew, Susan McGrath, Barton Shaw, Jim SoRelle, Charles Vincent, Cooper Thompson, Michael K. Honey, Charles W. McKinney, Jr., Jacquelyn Dowd Hall, Pete Daniel, Ira Berlin, George M. Fredrickson, and Sharon Thomason. I am especially grateful to K.K. Snyder, Pete de Lissovoy, William G. Anderson, Penny Patch, Jack Chatfield, Julian Bond, Emilye Crosby, Hasan Jeffries, Richard P. Weichert, Mary Sterner Lawson, Jamil Zainaldin, Susan O'Donovan, Deanna Weber, Khalil Muhammad, Nyota Tucker, Elizabeth Brown, and Herbert and Connie Phipps who read all or parts of the manuscript and made corrections and useful suggestions. I also wish to thank photographers Danny Lyon, Todd Stone, and Adrian Jenkins (who has preserved the work of Benjamin Cochran); and special thanks to Cathy Cowdrey for her graphic design work, and to ACRI Executive Director W. Frank Wilson, ACRI Museum Administrator Irene L. Turner, and the ACRI Board members for their encouragement and support.

Finally, a project of this magnitude could not have happened without the financial support of four pillars of Albany's business community—a hospital, a brewery, a bank, and a philanthropist—and the Georgia Humanities Council (GHC). When Phoebe Putney Memorial Hospital CEO Joel Wernick heard the story of Francis Flagg Putney's role in organizing the march that culminated in the Camilla Massacre and that Putney himself suffered a gunshot wound, he was sold on the project. Putney, a white carpetbagger, remained in Dougherty County for the rest of his long life and made the initial philanthropic gift that created the hospital named after his mother a century ago. Tim Dill of MillerCoors Albany Brewery and Len Dorminey of HeritageBank of the South also quickly saw the value of this project and together they matched Phoebe's gift. Jane Willson stepped in near the end of the project to insure that all our remaining costs were covered. Their support covers the cost of producing this publication so that all revenue from sales goes directly to the support of ACRI. When GHC President Jamil Zainaldin read the manuscript, he recognized its importance, and offered the GHC's support in promoting the book throughout Georgia and elsewhere. For the support of our sponsors and copublisher, ACRI is most grateful.

table of contents

1

When white settlers brought enslaved Africans and African Americans to southwest Georgia to grow cotton in the 19th century, they were not entering a virgin wilderness, but one that had been occupied and cultivated by Native Americans for centuries. In 1814, the southwest corner of the state was taken from the Lower Creek Indians by the Treaty of Fort Jackson ending the Creek War. The state of Georgia surveyed the land and by means of a lottery in 1820 gave it away in 250-acre parcels to white state residents. The idea was to reduce land speculation and develop on the Georgia frontier a society dominated by small white farmers. But rich cotton planters in the central and eastern parts of the state and in the Carolinas began buying up these parcels and

Among those planters bringing enslaved workers to southwest Georgia were some of the richest men in the state, including Joseph Bond of Macon and Hartwell Hill Tarver of Twiggs County. By the time of his death in 1858, Bond had amassed eight plantations in Lee and Dougherty counties worked by over 500 African Americans. The total value of his southwest Georgia land and enslaved labor was approximately $1 million. Like Bond, Hartwell Hill Tarver never permanently resided in southwest Georgia and his 2,700-acre plantation near Albany with 18 slaves in 1850, worth $25,000, was just a fraction of his statewide wealth. But three children of this Virginia-born absentee planter did make their homes and wealth in southwest Georgia. When his eldest son, Paul E.

SLAVERY AND THE ORIGINS OF THE SOUTHWEST GEORGIA FREEDOM STRUGGLE, 1814-1865

assembling thousand-acre and larger plantations to grow cotton, the real money crop in 19th-century Georgia. To work these plantations, the planters brought in large gangs of enslaved Africans and African Americans. Between initial settlement in the 1820s and emancipation in 1865, tens of thousands of African Americans were forcibly moved or sold to southwest Georgia. By 1836, when Nelson Tift established the town of Albany, cotton and corn were already the major crops of this region. By 1840, African American slaves outnumbered whites in the Albany area and by 1860 they comprised three-quarters of the Dougherty County population. On the eve of the Civil War, southwest Georgia's 63,000 bondsmen made up 54 percent of the region's population. In 1864, Judge Richard Clark told Governor Joseph E. Brown that southwest Georgia was one "vast negro Quarter."

Tarver, died in 1858, his 5,000 acres and 122 bondsmen were sold at auction and brought in close to $250,000.

The thousands of African Americans transplanted to the southwest Georgia frontier were uprooted from their families and communities on plantations or in towns in central and eastern Georgia, the Carolinas and as far away as the Chesapeake region. Even when slaves came as families, they were forced to leave communities and the support networks they had built there. Philip Joiner, a Virginia slave, was in his teens when he was moved to Dougherty County. Virginia-born Wilkins Tarver may have come as an enslaved infant with Hartwell Hill Tarver when the latter moved from Virginia to Georgia in 1816. Wilkins belonged to Hartwell's son Paul when Paul died in 1858. After Paul's widow, Cinderella Tarver, married Dr. Charles P. Heartwell, Wilkins Tarver became Heartwell's property.

OVER 500 NEGROES FOR SALE.

IN pursuance of the Will of Joseph Bond, late of the city of Macon, we will offer for sale before the Court House door, in Albany, Georgia, on the first Tuesday (the 3d day) in January next, over

500 Negroes!

belonging to said Estate.

These Negroes are all under good discipline—climatized to the country—well trained to the cultivation of corn and cotton, and are as likely a gang as will ever be offered again, perhaps, in any of the States South. In the lot there are several good Carpenters, Blacksmiths, and Wagon makers.

The terms of sale will be made known on the day, and the sale will be continued to each successive day.

And also, on Monday following, we will offer for sale all the remaining personal and perishable property of said deceased, consisting of a fine lot of Mules, Working-oxen, Cattle, Hogs, Plantation Blacksmith and Carpenter's Tools, and other fixtures, Household and Kitchen Furniture, and all the Corn, Fodder, Oats, and other provisions on hand at the time of sale. The sale will commence at the Fowltown Plantation, and be continued from day to day to the other plantations.

THOS. H. MOUGHON, } Ex'rs.
WM. S. MOUGHON, }
HENRIETTA S. BOND, Executrix.

Nov. 17, 1859.   34—

Advertisement for Joseph Bond Estate sale of slaves, one of the largest in American history. Albany Patriot, December 15, 1859

Twenty-Five Dollars Reward.

RUNAWAY from the subscriber about the 30th June last, a negro man by the name of Lewis, about 26 or 27 years of age, yellow complexion, about 5 feet, 3 inches high, and weighs nearly 140 pounds, quick spoken, his upper eye-lids seem to be puffed, his beard mostly grows upon his upper lip and the point of his chin. He is a negro of considerable intelligence and has a good countenance. Any person taking up said negro and delivering him to the subscriber living in Lee county, about four miles above Albany, shall receive the above reward; or if confined in any safe jail so that I can get him, I will give twenty dollars reward.

MOSES B. TISON.

January 13, 1849.   40 3t

Advertisement for fugitive enslaved man named Lewis from Lee County. Albany Patriot, January 27, 1849

Many of the African Americans forced to move to southwest Georgia were young. Slaves between the ages of 15 and 30 were the most productive and the most fertile—raising more cotton and increasing the owner's capital investment by bearing children. By 1860, 57 percent of enslaved southwest Georgians were age 18 and younger while only 12 percent were age 50 and older.

In addition to producing southwest Georgia planters and their enslaved workers, Virginia was also home to plantation overseers who made the move south. A good example was Paul Tarver's overseer, Littleton Phipps, who came from Brunswick County, Virginia, home of Paul's father and of his widow Cinderella's second husband, Charles P. Heartwell. Phipps ended up on the southwest Georgia frontier in the 1830s. In 1850 when he worked as Paul Tarver's overseer, he owned seven slaves, four of whom comprised his immediate family. His life partner, Mary Jane Phipps (1815-1900) was a woman of color and mother of their three children. When freedom came in 1865, Littleton and Mary Jane married and by the time he died in 1873, they were the parents of eight children. Chief Judge of the Court of Appeals of Georgia Herbert Phipps of Albany is Littleton Phipps's great-great-grandson.

Littleton and Mary Jane Phipps's interracial relationship was the exception to the rule in antebellum southwest Georgia. The region had a reputation for its brutality and racial exploitation of slave labor. An ex-slave in Dougherty County, reflecting three decades after slavery's end, declared, "This land was a little Hell. . . . I've seen niggers drop dead in the furrow, but they were kicked aside, and the plough never stopped." Enslaved southwest Georgians worked six days a week from sunup to sundown and sometimes after dark and on Sundays. The slaveholding planters' goal of profits from cotton production drove the oppressive labor system on many plantations in the region.

Clayborn Gantling, an enslaved teenager in Terrell County when slavery ended in 1865, was old enough to witness and to recall many years later the routine harshness of slave life in southwest Georgia. Children worked toting water to the older workers in the field, tending the cattle and sheep, and a variety of other chores. A horn was blown every morning to wake the hands, all of whom had to be in the field working at sunrise. Tardy workers "would be whipped with whips and leather strops." He remembered a woman on his plantation who "was beat until she could hardly get along. . . [and] she had to work along till she got better." Such images of cruelty and barbarity were seared in the minds of many enslaved southwest Georgians.

African Americans resisted slavery in many ways. Some workers engaged in silent sabotage including breaking equipment and tools, harming livestock, feigning illness, and slowing the pace of work when out of sight of the overseer. The ultimate form of resistance was armed rebellion, but this was relatively rare in the U.S. and never occurred in antebellum southwest Georgia. But a number of brave bondsmen challenged the system by running away— stealing themselves (i.e., their master's property). They were running for their freedom and in some ways they can be

where he had been purchased. Henry, a 23-year-old Lee County slave, was thought to be headed to Beaufort, S.C., where his former owner lived.

Some enslaved men fled to escape further physical abuse. Runaway advertisements often described identifying scars or marks on fugitives. Tombo had "marks from the whip, which show that he had been badly flogged." Also bearing the marks of the whip on his back was an 80-year-old "African negro" named Cooke, who spoke "very broken English" and who may have been the oldest runaway in southwest Georgia.

Some African American fugitives were persistent in their determination to be free. In June 1851 Ralph and John fled their master William Stegall of Albany heading for North Carolina. They were apparently caught and returned to Stegall who sold Ralph to Nelson Tift. The following January, Tift was advertising for his six-foot-tall "dark copper-colored man" who had run away again and was assumed to be heading home to North Carolina.

On the eve of the Civil War, southwest Georgia's 63,000 bondsmen made up 54 percent of the region's population. In 1864, Judge Richard Clark told Governor Joseph E. Brown that southwest Georgia was one "vast negro Quarter."

considered the first southwest Georgia freedom fighters.

An analysis of advertisements appearing in Georgia newspapers between 1835 and 1861 indicate that 9 out of 10 southwest Georgia runaway slaves were men. African American men were much more likely than women to have gone off the plantation for work related activity, such as running errands to the local town, and they were more familiar with the terrain. Reflecting the region's youthful slave population, three out of four southwest Georgia runaways were under 30.

A number of runaways headed towards their former homes. Twenty-three-year-old Ralph ran away from Albany and was thought to be headed towards North Carolina where he had been bought the previous winter. Lewis, age 23, also fled Albany and was considered to be going to Savannah "where he was formerly owned." Twenty-year-old Tombo with a "low-country brogue" left his owner in Dougherty County for Charleston, S.C.,

Another persistent African American named January fled his owner's Baker County plantation in May 1834 and headed for Columbia, S.C., where he grew up. He was captured and held in the Sandersville jail. Determined to be free, January broke out of jail and was still on the run months later. We do not know if Ralph or January ever secured their freedom, if they were captured, or if they ended up like the anonymous runaway who, in July 1852 drowned in the Flint River fleeing for his freedom.

Georgia law made it illegal to educate African Americans and with good reason from the slaveholder's perspective. An enslaved person who was able to write could forge a pass or permit that would help him escape. Two of Reuben S. Williams's bondsmen in Albany fled in April 1861 about the time the Confederates bombarded Fort Sumter thus commencing the Civil War. Both Ben Sykes and George were literate. George was "very intelligent, writes with a pen, performs well on the violin, and may have written his own permit for his passage" on the railroad from Albany. Ben Sykes was a 35-year-old mulatto carpenter, "a very intelligent boy, and can read and write." Williams thought Sykes was lurking in Dougherty, Lee, or Baker counties "where his acquaintants reside, and is no doubt endeavoring to write himself a pass" to "escape to a free State and take others with him."

The freedom Ben Sykes and Ralph strove for was experienced by a handful of African Americans in southwest Georgia. Unlike some other parts of the Deep South, southwest Georgia was not home to a substantial free black community. In 1860, all but eight of Dougherty County's 6,088 African Americans were enslaved. To be black in Dougherty County meant to be a slave. The most notable free black to work in the Albany area was Horace King, the former slave whose master emancipated him in 1846. King had developed a reputation as a master bridge builder in the Deep South. When Nelson Tift

wanted to build his toll bridge across the Flint River in the 1850s, he turned to Horace King who built not only the covered crossing but also the Bridge House. The building has survived the ravages of time and serves today as Albany's Welcome Center.

The 1850s saw a significant increase in sectional tensions between North and South over slavery, particularly its expansion to western territories. Southerners argued that slavery's future depended on its expansion. To halt slavery's growth would eventually doom it. Slaveholders had a significant capital investment in their human property. In 1860, the average enslaved person in the Albany area was worth $1,000. Some strong young men or skilled artisans were worth much more. In late 1859, Paul E. Tarver's bondsmen Shad and Joe Wilkinson were sold for $2,100 and $2,000 respectively. It is little wonder then that whites in southwest Georgia were terrified at the thought of a Republican victory in the 1860 presidential election. Although the Republican Party did not advocate the abolition of slavery

Antebellum southwest Georgia . . . had a reputation for its brutality and racial exploitation of slave labor.

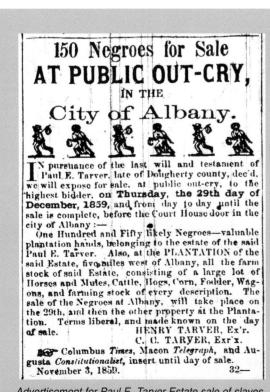

Advertisement for Paul E. Tarver Estate sale of slaves.
Albany Patriot, December 15, 1859

in the South, southerners felt Republican candidate Abraham Lincoln's victory would lead to the peculiar institution's extinction. So one by one, southern states held secession conventions, withdrew from the Union, and formed the Confederate States of America to better protect southern ownership of human property. Ironically, the southern attack on Fort Sumter in April 1861 precipitated the Civil War which ultimately destroyed the institution of slavery.

By recent standards (e.g., Vietnam, Iraq, and Afghanistan) the Civil War was relatively short, lasting only four years. But it was an intense four years during which 750,000 men died in a struggle that forever changed U.S. society and its federal government. While the war devastated and changed many southern communities, its impact on southwest Georgia was minimal. This was due largely to the lack of military action here. Southwest Georgia's contribution to the war effort was providing white men to fight and die on the battlefield and using black workers to grow provision crops to feed those southern soldiers and sailors.

In the great tidal wave of patriotism that engulfed the South in the spring of 1861, southwest Georgia had no difficulty offering up its young men as cannon fodder, but the region's planters were reluctant to switch from cotton to corn and wheat crops for the troops. Making great wealth had been a major reason for the expansion of cotton production using slave labor—why should a war which many southerners figured would be won quickly disturb the goose that laid the golden egg?

As the war dragged on into 1862, however, many white nonslaveholders wondered why they were asked to make the ultimate sacrifice while their rich planter neighbors refused to switch from cotton to grain crops. The Georgia legislature finally passed a law limiting the amount of cotton a grower could plant to three acres for each worker. Still, a large planter with 100 slaves could

Ten Dollars Reward.

RAN AWAY from the subscriber, (living in Baker county, Ga.) on the 12th May last, a negro boy named JANUARY — sometimes calls himself JACK. He is about 5 feet 6 or 7 inches high; slender made, and has a scar on one of his heels occasioned by the bite of a dog; his front teeth black, and when agitated stutters or stammers. He had on when he left common country homespun shirt and pantaloons, a black fur hat—also a round-about and pantaloons of blue striped janes. He was caught and lodged in Sandersvile jail, and there broke out, and I have never heard of him since. I expect he has made his way to Columbia, (S. C.) where he was raised, or towards Charleston.

BENJAMIN L. GREENWOOD.
October 27   5t

☞ The Charleston Courier, and Columbia Telescope, will publish the above once a week for six weeks, and forward their accounts to this office for payment.

Advertisement for fugitive enslaved man named January from Baker County. *Georgia Constitutionalist (Augusta), January 1, 1835*

> A number of brave bondsmen challenged the system by running away—stealing themselves (i.e., their master's property). They were running for their freedom and in some ways they can be considered the first southwest Georgia freedom fighters.

plant 300 acres in cotton. In addition, he did not have to perform military service as slaveholders with 20 or more slaves were exempt from the new Confederate conscription law. Although many Georgians thought too much cotton was still being planted after 1862, the law limiting cotton production did force most growers to shift to grain and other crops. Corn production in southwest Georgia increased significantly and the region soon became the Confederacy's breadbasket.

One justification by planters for their reluctance to shift from cotton to grain was that such change might affect control of their slave property. Change like that could undermine the very institution they were fighting to preserve. But the war continued to bring change and enslaved southwest Georgians looked for every opportunity to resist the system. Few went as far as Nelson, Sam, and George, the three African Americans who were hanged with a white man, John Vickery, when their insurrection

conspiracy was discovered in Brooks County in August 1864. More change came when planters along the Georgia coast, in anticipation of Sherman's March to the Sea, moved their human property to southwest Georgia, a safe distance from the warfront, thus increasing the African American population here.

All this change weakened the system of slavery as African Americans were emboldened to resist planter control in large and small ways. Still, when the war finally ground to a halt with Confederate defeat in the spring of 1865, slavery remained very much in place. Lincoln's 1863 Emancipation Proclamation had little effect in southwest Georgia as Union troops did not make it to this region to implement it. By the end of April 1865 the war was over and Lincoln was dead, yet enslaved southwest Georgians were still planting the fields under their owner's or his overseer's direction and whip.

This Is a White Man's Government" published two weeks before the Camilla Massacre. Harp..., 1868

2

If southwest Georgia planters were unhappy with the changes to their farming operations wrought by the Civil War, they were miserable with the cataclysmic consequence of defeat—emancipation of their slave labor force, which came with the arrival of Union troops in May 1865 and the beginning of Reconstruction. The misery of the former slave owner, however, was the joy of the new freedman. Southwest Georgia freedmen exercised their new liberty in numerous ways. Some abandoned the plantations for the freer urban environment of Albany. Others negotiated with their former owners the terms of their agricultural labor contracts, now required by a new federal agency called the Freedmen's Bureau. Within months of emancipation, African Americans began establishing independent churches and schools in Dougherty County staffed

west Dougherty County. The following spring, planter and future governor Alfred Holt Colquitt complained to the local bureau official in Albany that freedmen in west Dougherty "drill every night with drums, guns & sticks marching through the quarter and firing by platoons."

In the minds of former slaveholders, it was bad enough that the Freedmen's Bureau required them to negotiate and sign annual contracts with their freedmen. Then came Radical Reconstruction which extended the right to vote to African American men. In 1867, registered freedmen went to the polls for the first time in Dougherty County and they chose one of their own—ex-slave Philip Joiner—to represent them in the state constitutional convention and the state legislature. The thought of former slaves voting and being elected to office

EMANCIPATION AND RECONSTRUCTION,
1865-1880

by African American clergymen and educators. Black political organizing ensued.

The hot spot for political organizing was the Whitlock Place in east Dougherty County, which a group of Wilkes County freedmen had rented to farm on their own in 1866. In addition to growing cotton, the Wilkes County freedmen held regular meetings to discuss improvements in labor conditions, securing the vote, and insuring their own physical protection from white assault and abuse. When planters heard rumors about their former slaves carrying arms as well as marching and drilling at political meetings, they petitioned the Freedmen's Bureau in the summer of 1866 to put a halt to such proceedings which, they claimed, "demoralized" their labor force. The bureau responded that freedmen had the same rights as whites to create organizations or associations that did not violate the law. Vindicated, freedmen expanded their political activity into central and

enraged many whites and in the first 11 months of 1868, 112 African Americans in southwest Georgia were killed or wounded by whites intending to kill them. When several hundred African Americans walked from south Dougherty County to attend a political rally in Camilla in September 1868, they were attacked when they entered the courthouse square. A dozen marchers were killed and more than 30 wounded, including white Republican leader Francis Flagg Putney. Putney, a carpetbagger from New England, would later become one of the largest landholders in Dougherty County and in 1911, founded the Phoebe Putney Memorial Hospital named after his mother. With Putney at the Camilla Massacre was black Republican leader Philip Joiner, who had earlier that month been expelled from the Georgia legislature with the other 28 African American representatives and three black senators.

The violence at Camilla worked—only two Republican freedmen dared to vote on Election Day.

Thomas Nast, "The Modern Samson," published two weeks after the Camilla Massacre. Harper's Weekly, *October 3, 1868*

Meanwhile, in Albany, the Democrats' major weapon was fraud. Prominent white citizens working at the polls put ballots in their pockets and dropped them on the floor, while others altered the Republican ballots into Democratic ones before putting them in the boxes. Despite the fact that black voters outnumbered white voters four to one in Dougherty County, and that black voters almost universally voted Republican, the southern white Democrats carried the election in Dougherty County by 150 votes. It was a similar story across the state as counties with black and thus Republican majorities produced Democratic results at the polls.

The violence and fraud in the 1868 campaign disturbed Republican congressmen in Washington who had allowed Georgia's restoration to the Union that summer, and they decided to return the state to military rule in 1869. The original 1868 legislature with its African American members was called back into session and Philip Joiner returned to Atlanta to represent the interest of Dougherty County, particularly its black majority. Other African Americans from Dougherty County followed him to the statehouse—Howard Bunts in 1877 and Ishmael Lonon in 1880. Each of these three freedom fighters demonstrated their leadership and courage at the Camilla

Massacre and in subsequent political campaigns where they faced violence and fraud on a regular basis.

These were turbulent times for many southwest Georgians, and yet for most people life went on—plantations had to be run and cotton picked; couples fell in love and got married. For most couples in the region, getting married and settling down was not a problem, but that was not the case with Sandy and Carrie Hall. Sandy was African American and Carrie was white. As Carrie explained in her letter to the Freedmen's Bureau in 1867, "Some two or three yeares ago I Became verry much Atached to this colord gentleman for whom my dissier grew stronger and stronger everry day of my life." "He was the only one on this earth that I dissierd for a Husband." So they got married but kept it a secret. Word got out in the white community, however, and Carrie heard "they are making grate talk of what they are going to do and my mind is in grate trouble fearing they may try to carry out some of theare planes." She wanted the Bureau to provide two notes for them explaining that no one had any rights, "law or Authority to interfeare with us." She needed two notes as her husband was living across the Chattahoochee River near Eufaula, Alabama, and she was in Georgetown, Georgia. Her husband had a contract and could not leave the plantation he was on until year's end. She couldn't stay with him as the whites there opposed interracial marriage, so she was staying with Sandy's uncle in Georgetown.

The local bureau agent forwarded Carrie's letter to his superior who responded that "it is not advisable to have this matter ventilated further if it can be avoided, but if the parties are molested they may have redress under the Civil Rights Bill" of 1866. We do not know what became of Sandy and Carrie Hall as they disappeared from the records. Regardless of their ultimate fate, their actions in 1867 demonstrated how timeless human emotions could transcend racial barriers even in extremely racist southwest Georgia.

Like most African Americans in the region, Sandy Hall made his living as a farm laborer on a cotton plantation. On most Dougherty County plantations in 1870, growers continued to use the same type of gang labor that was practiced during slavery. In fact the majority of Dougherty freedmen (96.5 percent of the

meant freedom from the control of a white employer or landlord and the independence needed to determine the type and amounts of crops one grew. Sharecroppers and renters paying cotton rent were required to grow cotton by their southwest Georgia landlords. And sharecroppers were closely supervised by their landlords. Both whites and freedmen knew the freedom and independence that came with black landownership—that is why African Americans wanted it and whites steadfastly opposed it. The Wilkes County colony of freedmen who came to Dougherty County in 1866 could not get anyone to sell them land to farm. The only way they were able to rent the Whitlock Place in east Dougherty was with the assistance of the Freedmen's Bureau which found an out-of-state landowner willing to rent them the plantation. Their experience with this experiment in black control of farming strengthened the resolve of Dougherty County planters to oppose the sale of farmland to African Americans. Six years after emancipation not a single acre

For most couples in the region, getting married and settling down was not a problem, but that was not the case with Sandy and Carrie Hall. Sandy was African American and Carrie was white.

black household heads engaged in agriculture) were farm laborers who worked for cash or share wages (not to be confused with sharecropping, share wages meant one worked for wages that were paid by a share of the crop as opposed to operating a one-horse sharecropping farm). In 1870, a number of white planters were still trying to make the old system work. "I am get[t]ing on slow farming," wrote an exasperated Henry Tarver to his wife, "I never saw the Negroes so hard to get off to work as they are this year every one complaining." Change gradually came in the 1870s as a number of planters gave in to freedmen's demands for sharecropping and began dividing their plantations up into small 40- or 50-acre farms to be sharecropped or rented. But something more radical than giving in to demands for sharecropping happened at Dr. Charles P. Heartwell's central Dougherty County plantation and happened earlier there than anywhere else in the county.

The ultimate demand of newly freed African Americans was landownership. To farm one's own land

of Dougherty farmland was owned by blacks. That was about to change.

In December 1871, Charles P. Heartwell sold 250 acres of his central Dougherty plantation to his former bondsman Wilkins Tarver for $1,000. Wilkins Tarver was born enslaved in Virginia around 1815 and belonged to Paul Tarver when the young planter died in 1858. Wilkins was appraised in early 1859 at $1,000. After Heartwell married Paul's widow he became Wilkins's new owner. At the time, Wilkins was reappraised and the 48-year-old slave had lost $250 in value and was listed as "unhealthy." Wilkins lived not only to see his freedom in 1865, but five years later, he and his wife Rachel were listed as owning $300 in personal property and living six doors down from his former owner. By the end of the 1871 harvest season, they had scraped together the $1,000 for Heartwell's southernmost 250-acre land lot that the planter had purchased nearly two years earlier for $1,250. The fact that he was selling at a loss suggests that the doctor was doing this more out of generosity than as a good business deal. The spare legal records do not state a motive for the transaction, but Heartwell had to know that he risked incurring the wrath of his fellow planters by selling a good-sized plot of farmland to a former slave.

A study of post-Reconstruction African American mobility and persistence in Dougherty County suggests that Dr. Heartwell stood out among the county's planters as having an exceptionally good relationship with his employees and tenants. Dougherty County tax digest data indicates an increase in black mobility within the county. Moving reflected African American control over their labor. When they were dissatisfied with a planter employer, freedmen moved to a new place the next year. The average persistence rate (i.e., the percentage of blacks who stayed on a plantation from year to year) for Dougherty County blacks on a sample of plantations between 1878 and 1888 was a mere 12.5 percent. African Americans on Heartwell's two plantations had the highest percentage rates for persistence in the Dougherty County sample—

50 and 31.8 percent. The next highest persistence rate was 21.2 percent on Alfred Holt Colquitt's Gillionville Plantation. Most plantations had persistence rates between 10 and 20 percent and six plantations had a 0 percent rate. The two Heartwell plantations stood out as exceptions to the rule of high mobility, suggesting that labor conditions there were significantly better than elsewhere in Dougherty County.

Charles P. Heartwell was a lonely pioneer in selling farmland to African Americans. Nine months after he sold a land lot to Wilkins Tarver, another white planter—Thomas T. Buttrell—gave a land lot away to two of his former bondsmen. Then in November 1873 Wilkins Tarver sold 50 acres in the northeast corner of his land lot to another former Heartwell slave, Vinson Toson, for $200. Vinson was born in Georgia in 1830 and was married to Bina Toson. Like Wilkins, they had belonged to Paul Tarver and were appraised in 1859 for $1000 (Vinson) and $400 (Bina). In 1870 Vinson Toson was living four doors from

Both whites and freedmen knew the freedom and independence that came with black landownership—that is why African Americans wanted it and whites steadfastly opposed it.

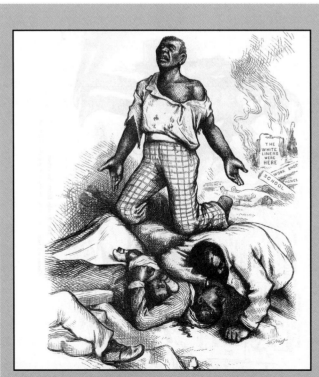

Thomas Nast, "Is *This* a Republican Form of Government? Is *This* Protecting Life, Liberty, or Property? Is *This* the Equal Protection of the Laws?" Harper's Weekly, September 2, 1876

Dr. Heartwell. Three years later, he was the proud owner of a 50-acre or one-horse farm, large enough to support him and his family. Vinson's acquisition doubled the number of black farmland owners in central Dougherty County. As late as 1874, Vinson and Wilkins and the two Buttrell beneficiaries were the only black farmland owners in the county. Slowly the number began to grow. In 1875, there were six black farmland owners in the county, but that number nearly quintupled over the next eight years. In 1883, there were 29 black farmland owners—20 of whom were in east Dougherty where the quality of soil was poorer and the land cheaper. Fifteen years later the number had increased to 51—still a tiny fraction of the county's 11,000 African Americans in 1898. Still for many whites this was 51 too many. Around 1898, a number of Dougherty County deeds began including restrictive covenant language precluding buyers from "sell[ing] said land to NEGROES."

The history of what happened to some black landowners in postemancipation southwest Georgia may be told through the story of Wilkins and Rachel Tarver and Vinson and Bina Toson. Less than a year after he sold 50 acres of his new farm to his friend Vinson Toson, Wilkins Tarver died on September 1, 1874. The next year, Zeke Tarver was listed as an agent on the Wilkins Tarver Estate place. Zeke, another former Heartwell slave, was 28 and probably Wilkins's son. Rachel and Zeke probably ran the 200-acre farm. In 1882, Rachel mortgaged the property to Hartwell H. Tarver for $400. These were tough times for Rachel and she did not pay back Hartwell H. Tarver the money she owed him. Hartwell sued Rachel and the court ordered a sheriff's sale. At the sale in September 1891, Sam Farkas, who went on to build a real estate empire, bought the Wilkins Tarver place for $250, thus ending black ownership of this farm.

Vinson and Bina Toson had better luck in holding on to their 50-acre farm. Vinson died without a will in January 1894, so in March Bina petitioned the Court of Ordinary (the probate court) to appraise Vinson's

Thomas Nast, "Worse Than Slavery." Harper's Weekly, October 24, 1874

The emergence of renting and sharecropping was an improvement over the gang labor system of farming that reminded [the freedmen] of slavery, but planters were learning how to exploit these new labor systems as well.

$300 estate and secure her widow's portion (a year's support to which she was entitled by law). Apparently because the estate was so small, the appraisers awarded her the entire estate left by Vinson: the horse, the cow and the calf, the wagon, 25 bushels of corn, two stacks of fodder, 30 bushels of cotton seed, the household and kitchen furniture, and most important, the 50 acres of land. As late as 1910, the farm remained in the hands of the Vinson Toson estate. Having learned from her probate experience with her husband's estate, Bina Toson made out a will so her family members would inherit what she wished.

With the end of Reconstruction and the beginning of the Jim Crow era, southwest Georgia freedmen faced an uncertain future. Violence and fraud limited their voting power in majority black counties, but in places like Dougherty County they continued to elect black men to represent them in the state legislature through 1881. The emergence of renting and sharecropping was an

improvement over the gang labor system of farming that reminded them of slavery, but planters were learning how to exploit these new labor systems as well. African Americans built their own churches, their own schools, their own burial societies, and fraternal organizations. By 1880, African Americans comprised 85 percent of the population in Dougherty County, but whites had most of the political and economic power in the region. Still, many black workers were able to exercise some choice in who their employers would be. In late December 1880, an Albany observer noted that many African Americans "appear to be unsettled in their places for another year. The roads of the county are lined with wagons, moving people from one plantation to another. We have never witnessed so much moving since '65 and '66 when everything was in an unsettled condition." Resistance to "the man" (i.e., the white man) continued to be a theme in the African American community as it entered the last decades of the 19th century.

Spring Plowing in Dougherty County. This and the other photographs in this chapter were made by A. Radclyffe Dugmore in Dougherty County in March 1901 to illustrate W.E.B. Du Bois's article, "The Negro As He Really Is," published in World's Work *2 (June 1901): 848-66.*

3

As African Americans continued to resist oppression in the late 19th century, white southwest Georgians added a new weapon to their arsenal of violence and fraud—the law. The Jim Crow era is distinguished by the codification into state and local law of white control over black life. One of the earliest examples of this abuse of law to re-exert mastership was the establishment of convict leasing in which the state basically rented out its expanding number of penitentiary prisoners to private contractors. Southwest Georgia planter Col. Benjamin G. Lockett took advantage of this new way of exploiting black labor and established penitentiary camps on three plantations in Dougherty County.

Life at the Lockett penitentiary camps was like slavery on steroids. In 1880, the three camps held a total of 162 prisoners, five of whom were white and six of whom were

were listed as dying of sunstroke. Col. Lockett's son, William Lockett, ran the Royston Place and was known to personally whip prisoners on the naked skin with a leather strap 30-40 times drawing blood. Travel on the roads near the camps was unsafe and innocent neighbors and passersby were "chased and bitten by the camp dogs, and . . . assailed and beaten by the convicts" often with the approval of the whipping bosses.

For eight years Benjamin Lockett ran these three hellholes, but abuse of prisoners continued long after he went out of business. In March 1901, the captain of the Dougherty County Misdemeanor Chain-Gang filed his monthly report indicating that a half dozen of his 23 prisoners got anywhere from five to fifteen licks for "not working."

JIM CROW ORIGINS TO WORLD WAR II,
1880-1941

women. To be a Lockett convict meant, practically speaking, to be an African American male. Felons and those convicted of misdemeanors were treated the same—awakened by 3:30 a.m. to begin 12 to 15 hours at hard labor and lights out at 9 p.m. The camps were rife with abuse and the Georgia Senate investigated the brutal behavior, particularly by the whipping bosses, in 1881. Jesse G. Youngblood, a guard on Lockett's Rawls Place in 1877-1878, stated "that on many occasions, while he was on guard, he saw the colored convicts . . . whipped unmercifully with a strap by the whipping boss, and on one occasion he witnessed one colored convict . . . whipped by Dick Pound, captain of the camp, until his skin was perfectly raw, and that while the whipping was being inflicted, the convict was held fast by six other convicts. That on several occasions he saw convicts severely whipped and made to work, after they had complained of being sick and unable to work." Prisoners on the Royston Place who died of overexertion and exhaustion in the fields

Violence and intimidation continued to be a weapon of choice to reduce black voting in southwest Georgia. A Blakely judge described the effectiveness of the Colomokee Nine in keeping African Americans from voting in the 1880s: "At one election . . . the members had appeared at the precinct in baseball suits, and each of them carried a baseball bat. They used for the ball the head of any Negro who tried to vote." Hand in hand with the violence came voter reform (i.e., disfranchisement) legislation beginning with the cumulative poll tax in 1877, the all-white primary in 1900, and literacy tests and property qualifications in 1908. By this time African American voting in southwest Georgia practically ceased and in 1915 there were only 28 blacks registered to vote in Albany.

At the same time whites were codifying African American disfranchisement, they began formalizing through the passage of Jim Crow laws the informal

One of the few African American store owners in Dougherty County, March 1901

segregation of the races that had been practiced in many places since emancipation. The first statewide Jim Crow law, passed in 1891, provided for separate cars on railroads. Cities and towns followed suit passing Jim Crow ordinances. When the new Union train station in Albany was built in 1913, it was designed with separate waiting rooms—one for white passengers and one for passengers of color. This made very physical the segregation required by Georgia law. This architecture of segregation is still visible today at the Thronateeska Heritage Center museum housed in the former Union station. Segregation—separation—apartheid: it was all about maintaining white supremacy by separating and thus denigrating people of color. This was the essence of the Jim Crow era.

Most African Americans in Jim Crow southwest Georgia worked as cotton farmers. White control in the Jim Crow era insured that few blacks became landowners. The majority eked out a living as sharecroppers or renters. Political control by whites meant that state and local laws reinforced white control and exploitation of black share-croppers. And when legal control was not enough, whites resorted to the extralegal and ultimate weapon of terror—lynching. In 1899 white terrorists known as "whitecappers"

in Early and Miller counties launched a campaign of killing African Americans and burning black property "to produce entirely white counties." Between 1880 and 1930, 122 African Americans, mostly men, were lynched in southwest Georgia.

Lynching victims were often accused of murder and rape. Dan Buck in Clay County was lynched in 1891 for attempted rape. Two lynching outbreaks in Lee County in 1899 resulted in the deaths of five African American men accused variously of rape, "wild talk," and "informing." In 1917, Jesse Stater was lynched in Brooks County for writing letters to a white girl. Brooks County, with 22 lynchings between 1880 and 1930, was the lynching capital of southwest Georgia and was the scene of one of the worst lynching atrocities in 1918. Mary Turner, an eight-month pregnant African American, age 21, had the temerity to say that if she discovered the names of those who had just lynched her husband she would report them to the authorities. The lynch mob returned for Mary, tied her upside down from a tree, poured gasoline and oil on her and set her afire burning off her clothes. Someone then sliced open her abdomen and the baby fell to the ground where it was stomped to death. Members of the mob then riddled Mary's body with bullets.

The barbarity of African American lynchings, as well as the more prosaic indignities of Jim Crow life, was all too familiar to the young Atlanta University Professor W.E.B. Du Bois. The first African American to receive a Harvard Ph.D., Du Bois spent his two- to three-month summer vacation in 1898 in Dougherty County researching African American life in the Georgia black belt. With two or three research assistants, Du Bois "visited nearly every colored family in the county," collecting data on 6,093 blacks who lived in the country district as well as 2,500 in Albany. The most important and famous result of his Dougherty County research was two chapters in his celebrated 1903 classic *The Souls of Black Folk*. In the Dougherty County chapters, Du Bois paints a devastating and depressing portrait of African American life in "the heart of the Black Belt," the "centre of those nine million men who are America's dark heritage from slavery and the slave-trade." "Below Macon," Du Bois observed, "the world grows darker; for now we approach the Black

African American life in the southwest Georgia black belt, Joseph Winthrop Holley moved there in 1903 and founded the Albany Bible and Manual Training Institute, basically a grammar school in its early years. By 1918 when the state took it over and renamed it Georgia Normal and Agricultural College, Holley had expanded its curriculum to the two-year college level. In 1943, it became Albany State College and offered the four-year baccalaureate degree. And today, Albany State University is the major institution of higher education in southwest Georgia.

Soon after the Civil War, African Americans broke away from the white controlled biracial churches they attended during slavery and created their own black churches. Mt. Zion Baptist Church in Albany started out in 1866 when blacks in the Albany Baptist Church broke off and formed the First Colored Baptist Church. In 1906 members of Mt. Zion built the church which became the home of the Albany Civil Rights Movement Museum in the 1990s. In 1888, a group of disgruntled Mt. Zion

Segregation—separation—apartheid: it was all about maintaining white supremacy by separating and thus denigrating people of color. This was the essence of the Jim Crow era.

Belt,—that strange land of shadows, at which even slaves paled in the past, and whence come now only faint and half-intelligible murmurs to the world beyond."

Du Bois described the depressing daily grind African American farm workers faced in Dougherty County: "Among this people there is no leisure class. . . . Here ninety-six per cent are toiling; no one with leisure to turn the bare and cheerless cabin into a home. . . . The toil, like all farm toil, is monotonous, and here there are little machinery and few tools to relieve its burdensome drudgery." "The land on the whole is still fertile, despite long abuse. For nine or ten months in succession the crops will come if asked: garden vegetables in April, grain in May, melons in June and July, hay in August, sweet potatoes in September, and cotton from then to Christmas. And yet on two-thirds of the land there is but one crop [cotton], and that leaves the toilers in debt."

In Jim Crow Georgia, African Americans continued to create their own religious, social, and educational institutions. Inspired by Du Bois's observations on

members broke away and established a new church, Shiloh Baptist Church, right across the street from their old church. These two churches became ground zero for civil rights mass meetings of the 1960s.

Southwest Georgians created and joined fraternal orders and benevolent societies. The headquarters of the Supreme Circle of Benevolence, one of the largest African American benevolent orders in the nation, was located in Albany. Albany businessman and Republican party man Joe H. Watson, Supreme Ruler of the order, turned the first shovelful of dirt at the December 1912 groundbreaking of the new $50,000 Supreme Circle Temple in Albany. The Union Aid Society had chapters throughout southwest Georgia and was presided over by Albany businessman C.W. King. East Albany grocer J.A. Pones founded the Pones Aiding Society in 1915 to help meet the medical and burial needs of struggling African Americans. Members held monthly meetings and paid dues and were guaranteed a decent burial. The Pones Aiding Society cemetery, adjacent to the

Albany State University campus, is now owned by Poteat Funeral Home.

The southwest Georgia African American leaders of these social and philanthropic self-help efforts, like Watson, Pones, and King, comprised a small elite of middle-class businessmen and professionals in the region's towns. Several black businessmen—like Deal Jackson and Bartow Powell—however, made their fortune in agriculture. Du Bois encountered both these men on his visit to Albany. Deal Jackson, who for 13 years brought in the first bale of cotton to market, owned 650 acres in 1898 with 11 tenants in Dougherty County. Bartow Powell was even wealthier. He took the money he made on government contracts dredging southwest Georgia rivers and bought land in Baker County. "He owned a barony—10,000 fertile acres" that had "fields of purpling cotton . . . villages of white and black tenants . . . school houses for both colors—it was a matter for rubbing your eyes," Du Bois exclaimed. Powell's turn-of-the-century Victorian bungalow in Albany still stands on the same block as the Albany Civil Rights Institute (see p. 92). Jackson and Powell grew rich, but did so at the cost of showing deference and humility in their business dealings with whites. These unusual men did not resist Jim Crow, but learned how to work the system to their advantage.

Deal Jackson and Bartow Powell were the exception to the rule. For most African Americans Jim Crow meant a life of grinding poverty working for "the man." Unlike Jackson and Powell, some African American businessmen and professionals could not ignore the plight of the poor black farmers who were often cheated and discriminated against by the local white elite. In Thomasville, Valdosta, and Albany, some responded by organizing local chapters of the NAACP in 1918 and 1919. Local whites viewed the NAACP, which opposed segregation and disfranchisement, with distrust and hatred. In those southwest Georgia counties with the highest lynching rates (Brooks, Early, Decatur, Mitchell and Lee) and with few or no middle

"Below Macon," Du Bois observed, "the world grows darker; for now we approach the Black Belt,—that strange land of shadows, at which even slaves paled in the past, and whence come now only faint and half-intelligible murmurs to the world beyond."

African American broom maker in Albany, March 1901

class blacks, African Americans did not establish local NAACP chapters until after World War II.

It is ironic that in counties where white hostility to the NAACP hindered chapter formation until the post-World War II era, 20 divisions of Marcus Garvey's Universal Negro Improvement Association (UNIA) were established in the 1920s. Garvey's black separatist ideology called for decolonization of Africa and establishment of a "strong and powerful Negro nation" there. Garvey's insistence on strong racial pride, belief in developing separate black economic institutions, and opposition to interracial sex formed the basis for most versions of the Black Power movements in the 20th century. Garveyism appealed to the poor and powerless, who viewed his back-to-Africa plans as the solution to the problem of living in a racist society controlled by whites.

The primarily middle-class NAACP opposed Garvey's back-to-Africa movement and his rejection of integration. In those rural southwest Georgia counties with little or no black middle class and no NAACP, black tenant farmers were attracted to Garvey's ideas and formed local divisions of the UNIA. More than half of the 34 divisions in Georgia in 1926 were in its southwest corner. Worth County, where tenant farmers complained of regular abuse by landlords, had five divisions, while Pelham and Camilla in Mitchell County each had a division. Divisions were often located in tiny communities like Ty Ty, Ray City, and Haylow. Even in counties with no UNIA divisions, like Terrell, Randolph, Dougherty, and Thomas, supporters sent money and letters of support that were published in the organization's weekly, the *Negro World*. Although white landlords strongly resisted the NAACP, they may have been less likely to oppose the UNIA, because it encouraged separation of the races.

A number of African Americans resisted oppression in southwest Georgia by simply leaving the region. During World War I and into the 1920s, large numbers of dissatisfied African American farmers boarded the train and left southwest Georgia for northern cities where employment was better and the racial climate an improvement over the South. Southwest Georgia migrants left those counties with the worst lynching rates and labor relations. Local landowners went to train stations in some communities and had their fleeing labor supply with northern tickets arrested on trumped up charges. A number of departing farm workers in Thomas, Mitchell, Early, Miller, and Calhoun counties bought tickets to Albany where they then purchased their tickets for Chicago, Philadelphia, and other northern cities. The result was the southwest Georgia black belt became paler over time, and by the 1950s, African Americans were no longer a majority of the population in Dougherty County.

As blacks were leaving southwest Georgia, whites from other parts of the country moved in during the 1940s. World War II was a turning point in this development. Many whites were exposed to southwest Georgia through service at military bases in Albany and Valdosta. The Second World War would also have a significant impact on race relations and the freedom struggle in southwest Georgia.

Saturday in turn-of-the-century Albany when, according to Du Bois, "the whole county disgorges itself upon the place, and a perfect flood of black peasantry pours through the streets."

African American cobbler in Albany, March 1901

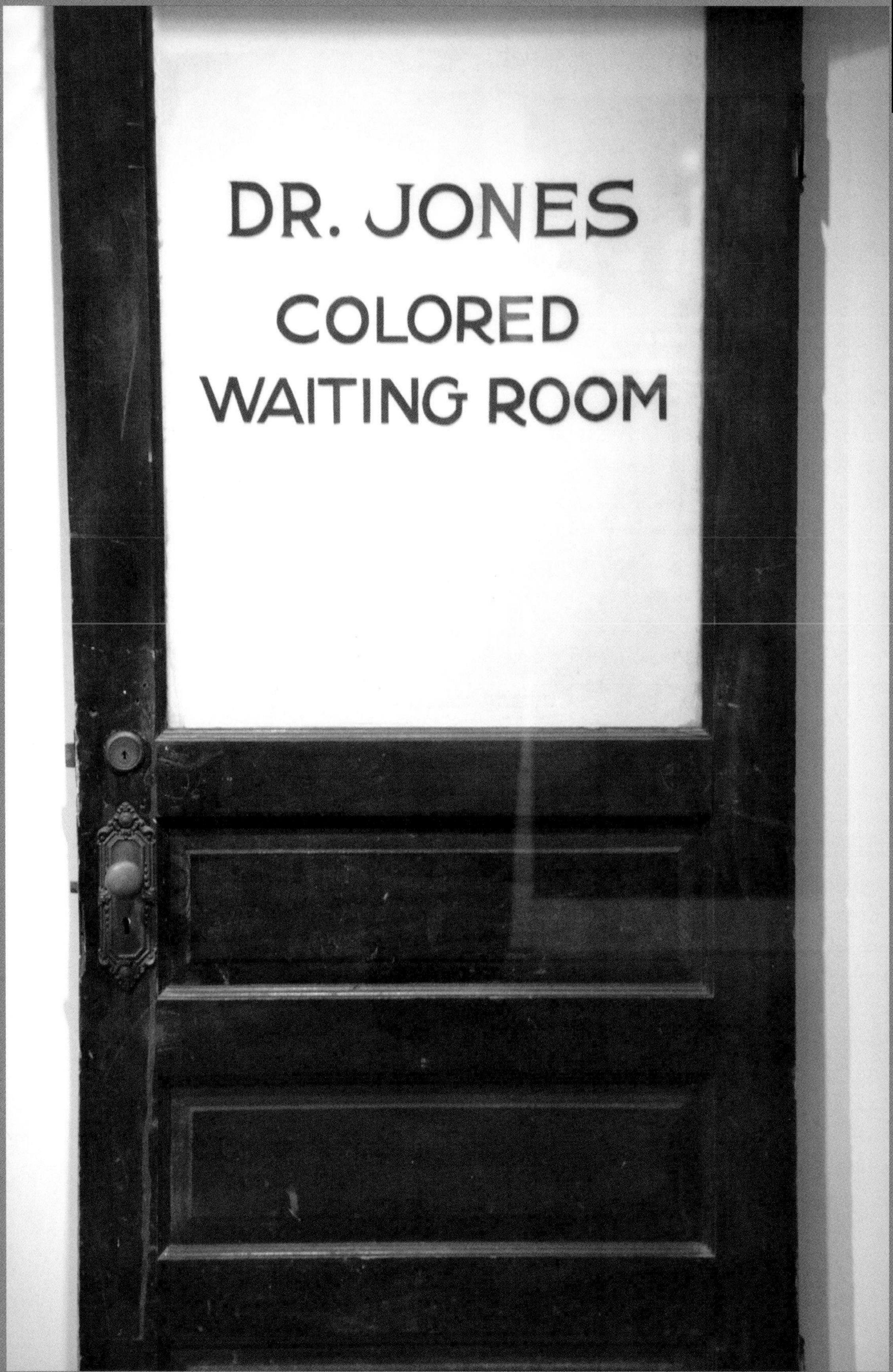
DR. JONES
COLORED
WAITING ROOM

4

World War II, the Korean War, and the Cold War had a significant impact on the struggle for civil rights in southwest Georgia. African American soldiers and civilians played important roles in the war effort, and when servicemen and women returned home after risking their lives in the cause of freedom, they encountered the same Jim Crow system they had left behind—a system that publicly humiliated and demeaned them because of their skin color. Having faced death in Europe and the Pacific, many of these courageous veterans challenged Jim Crow at home.

African Americans in southwest Georgia enthusiastically endorsed the war effort. They entered the armed services and by the last months of the war, over 1,100 African Americans from Albany alone had served in the military. In 1945, 68 students and eight faculty at historically black

native William Levi Dawson, had been elected and sworn in on January 3, 1943, as congressman for the first district of Illinois. This African American Democrat would continue to represent Chicago in the U.S. House of Representatives until his death in 1970. Like a number of southwest Georgia blacks, he found success by leaving the region earlier in the century. For Dawson and others, Albany was, in the words of Albany African American newspaperman A.C. Searles, "one step from Hell." Hell, he explained, was neighboring Baker County.

Three weeks after Congressman Dawson was sworn into office, 30-year-old African American Robert Hall encountered the hell of Baker County. Baker County Sheriff Claude Screws had a grudge against Hall and arrested him at his home late at night on the charge of

From World War II to the Cold War: the Struggle Continues,
1941-1959

Albany State College (ASC) were in military service. The college also provided military housing for servicemen and was the residential headquarters for African American WACS in south Georgia and north Florida. In the nation's officer corps were several men who had attended Albany's African American schools.

African American civilians in southwest Georgia also supported the war effort. Albany educator Ruth Kimbrough played a key role in setting up an African American USO Center on Mercer Street which provided an opportunity for local women to meet black servicemen stationed at Turner Army Air Force Base. A local War Finance Committee, in charge of the war bond drives among African Americans, was cochaired by ASC President Aaron Brown and businessman Frank Tarver, and southwest Georgia blacks purchased their share of war bonds.

In the middle of World War II, southwest Georgia African Americans learned that one of their own, Albany

stealing a tire. Screws and two officers handcuffed Hall and drove him to the courthouse. At the courthouse square they beat Hall with their fists and an eight-inch long, two-pound "solid-bar blackjack" and continued to pummel him for 15 to 30 minutes. They then dragged the unconscious victim into the jail before an ambulance came and carried Hall to a hospital where he died. Screws and the two officers were indicted for violating Hall's civil rights and convicted in federal court in Albany by an all-white jury. The conviction was upheld by an appeals court and brought before the U.S. Supreme Court in October 1944. Meanwhile back in Baker County, Sheriff Screws ran for reelection and defeated his closest competitor three to one. The following spring, the Supreme Court over-turned the sheriff's conviction, arguing that although it was clear that the three officers had intended to kill Hall, it had not been proved that they had "willfully" deprived him of his civil rights.

The Criterion Club, founded in 1947, was actively engaged in African American voter registration efforts. C.W. King is at the right end of the first row. *AE Jenkins Photography*

While the federal jury in October 1943 was convicting Sheriff Screws in Albany, a new African American leader was settling in as the second president of Albany State College. Aaron Brown, who had served as principal of Moultrie's Negro high school, was finishing up his Ph.D. at the University of Chicago in the spring of 1943 when he was offered the ASC presidency. ASC was going through a major transition that year as the Board of Regents terminated Georgia Normal and Agricultural College's founder Joseph Winthrop Holley, changed its name to Albany State College, and expanded it from a two-year to a four-year institution. Brown proved himself an able administrator who stood by his principles. Unlike his predecessor, he publicly opposed racial discrimination and encouraged ASC faculty and students to join the NAACP. Within months of his arrival in Albany, he asked the Savannah branch of the NAACP Youth Council to form an ASC chapter. In 1945, Brown asked Albany city commissioners to address the problem of white men speeding through the ASC campus, a grievance that irritated students over the years.

The year before Aaron Brown took over the leadership of ASC, two white couples founded an interracial Christian cooperative, Koinonia Farm, in nearby Sumter County and began their own quiet challenge to Jim Crow. Koinonia soon encountered local opposition to its support of conscientious objectors during the war and its treatment of local African American members as equals. Eventually because of its integration efforts, Koinonia incurred the wrath of the

Ku Klux Klan and many white southwest Georgians who instituted a boycott of the farm and vandalized and attacked the religious agrarian cooperative. During the heyday of the southwest Georgia civil rights movement in the early 1960s, Koinonia served as a respite for exhausted civil rights workers who came to Koinonia for rest and relaxation before returning to the battlefront in Albany and Americus.

Black life in Albany was the subject of study by two African American Ph.D.s in the Jim Crow era. The most famous was W.E.B. Du Bois's *The Souls of Black Folk* (1903). Less well-known, but nearly as important was Aaron Brown's *The Negro in Albany* (1945), a 70-page examination of the African American community in the last year of World War II. The ASC president, busy with reorganizing the college administration, expanding the size of the student body, and promoting the war effort, managed to collect data on African Americans and their housing, education, religion, business, and social and political activities in Albany. Almost a half-century after Du Bois's observations, Brown's reflections on the state of apartheid in Albany reveal how much had changed in 50 years as well as the continued harm caused by living in a Jim Crow society.

While half of Albany's 25,000 residents in 1945 were African American, they owned a mere four percent of the city's real estate value. The city's Housing Authority owned three public housing projects for low-income residents. Only one of the projects—the O.B. Hines Homes with 56 apartments—was for African Americans. Aaron Brown called Albany's African American schools "deplorable." There was severe overcrowding in the city's five black schools, one of which had been destroyed in the 1940 tornado. Albany's first public high school for African Americans was established only in 1928. The county schools outside Albany were mostly "one-teacher schools."

Brown counted 125 African American businesses in 1945, employing 352 persons and ranging from a casket manufacturer to grocery stores to service industry and professionals. There were a few rich African Americans in southwest Georgia in the 1940s. Wealthy farmer Dave Jackson owned more than 1,000 acres near Adel and was known by African American leaders as far away as Mississippi. Dr. Joseph Howard Griffin of Bainbridge was as much a businessman as a surgeon. In 1930 he established his own infirmary and his medical practice soared. Twenty years later he built with his own money—$250,000—the largest private hospital for African Americans in Georgia. He made his fortune by having his patients sign security deeds on their

cooks, and yardmen. President Brown made it clear that the reason most common laborers were not promoted to skilled trades was "due entirely to race rather than to merit."

One industry where southwest Georgia African Americans saw some progress was the meat-packing business, largely due to aggressive union organizing. Albany had become an important meat processing center with a million-dollar Cudahy plant that in 1941 had blacks and whites working alongside each other and earning equal pay. In 1944 an African American union organizer, John Henry Hall, came south and organized packinghouse workers in Moultrie.

Jim Crow may have been wounded in the meat-packing plants of Albany, Moultrie, and Tifton, but he was very much alive elsewhere in southwest Georgia. African American leaders saw voting as the key to challenge Jim Crow and they looked to the NAACP for direction. During World War II, only one of Georgia's six NAACP branches was in southwest Georgia, but the branch in Albany was one of the largest in the state. In 1944, it

Like Deal Jackson and Bartow Powell of an earlier generation, Joe Griffin was rich, black, and powerful, but the success of each of them in Jim Crow southwest Georgia . . . required accommodation, i.e., wearing the mask when necessary in interacting with whites.

property and then foreclosing on them when they missed a payment. In addition, he carried on an illegal abortion practice based on a ready supply of coeds in nearby Tallahassee's Florida State University and Florida A & M University as well as black women in the Bainbridge area. Providing venereal disease "treatments" to white and black patients also proved lucrative. Like Deal Jackson and Bartow Powell of an earlier generation, Joe Griffin was rich, black, and powerful, but the success of each of them in Jim Crow southwest Georgia—whether at the beginning or the middle of the 20th century—required accommodation, i.e., wearing the mask when necessary in interacting with whites. Thus the same Joe Griffin who was deferential to whites in public could be seen at church meetings urging African Americans to register to vote and to pay their poll taxes so they could cast their ballots.

Most black professionals in southwest Georgia were not rich and powerful and comprised a tiny sliver of the black population. The greatest percentage of African American workers in Albany was engaged in domestic service as maids,

funded the defense of an African American soldier accused of attacking a bus driver who had assaulted the serviceman. The latter war years and early postwar period was an era of comparative political moderation led by Governor Ellis Arnall who secured repeal of the poll tax. During his tenure, the federal courts abolished the whites-only primary in Georgia. In 1945, Aaron Brown reported less than 1,000 African American voters in Albany. As the war wound down and African American veterans returned to southwest Georgia, a number of them joined the Albany NAACP and others helped establish five branches elsewhere in the region, including Donaldsonville and Miller County.

To be an open member of the NAACP was a radical act in 1945 in rural southwest Georgia. Independence of white control was critical for these NAACP members. Courageous leaders, like black landowner D. Ulysses Pullum, who organized the Terrell County NAACP in the early 1940s, often found themselves without many followers, so terrified were African Americans in counties like these. Conservative black leaders in some communities, like Camilla, actually organized to oppose the local NAACP because they feared a change in the status quo.

The 1946 election witnessed a violent resurgence of white supremacy in southwest Georgia. In Taylor County, African American veteran Private Maceo Snipes was warned not to vote. He ignored the threats, voted, and three days later was killed by 10 white men on his front porch. Elsewhere, black union organizers were chased out of the region and the leadership ranks of the rural NAACP branches were ravaged. The lack of leadership in Early County, for example, resulted in its NAACP branch going dormant in the early 1950s. The moderation of the mid-1940s ended with the white supremacist violence. The 1948 election ushered in the Herman Talmadge years of arch-segregation and with it the explosion in Ku Klux Klan membership. During the Second World War there were only 12 Klaverns statewide; by 1949 there were 110 Klaverns throughout the state, a number of them in

Meanwhile, in 1947 NAACP supporter ASC President Aaron Brown hired a new athletic director who put his energy into bringing hometown African American athlete Alice Coachman (1923-2014) back from Tuskegee Institute

Georgia Normal and Agricultural College President Joseph Winthrop Holley with graduating students before his retirement in 1943. Albany State University

Courageous leaders, like black landowner D. Ulysses Pullum, who organized the Terrell County NAACP in the early 1940s, often found themselves without many followers, so terrified were African Americans in counties like these.

southwest Georgia. The Klan visited Terrell County's D.U. Pullum frequently, and in 1948 cross burnings in Valdosta lowered black voter turnout in Lowndes County.

Despite the vicious white backlash, African American resistance to Jim Crow and white supremacy did not end everywhere in southwest Georgia. The desegregated military bases in Albany, Columbus, and Valdosta were islands of racial moderation. African American leadership in Albany also stood up to challenge racial oppression. In 1947, a group of black letter carriers formed the Criterion Club, which created a local Voters League to expand African American voting in Albany. As a result, the 1950 election in Albany saw 800 black voters turn out. When Rosa Lee Ingram, a black sharecropper and widowed mother of 12, was convicted in 1948 for the self-defense murder of a white man near Ellaville, Albany NAACP President E.D. Hamilton called her death sentence a "legal lynching" and set up a local branch of the Legal Defense Fund created by the national NAACP for Ingram's appeals.

where she was matriculating and making a name for herself as a potential Olympic competitor. Coachman transferred to ASC and in 1948 was a member of the U.S. Olympic team at the London games. When she won the gold medal for the high jump competition, she became the only American woman in 1948 and the first African American woman ever to bring home Olympic gold. Following a 175-mile motorcade from Atlanta to Albany, Coachman's hometown welcomed her in Jim Crow fashion at a ceremony at the Municipal Auditorium with segregated seating.

In 1951 another African American daughter of southwest Georgia began a journey that would eventually attract a different type of national and international notice. Albany midwife Mary Coley met filmmaker George Stoney, who had been commissioned by the Georgia Department of Public Health to write, direct, and produce an educational film for granny midwives, African American women who delivered babies in the rural South. The film *All My Babies*, starring Mary Coley, was distributed to health departments and medical and nursing schools in this country and to health ministries and medical schools in various Asian, African, Latin American and European nations and colonies. In 2002, the film—a work of cinematic art and a document of Jim Crow southwest Georgia—was denoted as "culturally, historically, or aesthetically significant" by the Library of Congress and selected for preservation in the United States Film Registry.

Five years after Alice Coachman had been honored on the city auditorium stage, ASC President Aaron Brown participated in a local Voters League public forum on that same stage in July 1953. The meeting had been organized by C.W. King, Sr., a founder of both the Criterion Club and the Voters League. Brown's role in the forum was minimal, that of introducing one of the speakers. The forum, however, was condemned by arch-segregationist editor James H. Gray in the *Albany Herald* as advocating Negro "bloc voting."

Albany. C.W. King, Sr.'s son, C.B. King, was admitted to the Georgia bar in 1953 and became the first African American attorney in the state outside Atlanta to accept civil rights cases. C.B. King and Atlanta-based Donald Hollowell became the state's leading civil rights attorneys by the late 1950s.

In 1954, the U.S. Supreme Court handed down its momentous *Brown v. Board of Education* decision outlawing school segregation. In southwest Georgia whites responded with a demand for massive resistance to school desegregation. In contrast there was little reaction by African Americans in the region. In 1955 the Valdosta NAACP was the only southwest Georgia NAACP branch to petition its local school board to comply with *Brown*.

The mid 1950s appeared bleak for African Americans in southwest Georgia. Massive resistance, the growth of the Ku Klux Klan, and the arch-segregationist voice of the new media king in Albany, James H. Gray, who controlled the major daily newspaper, a radio station, and the

Massive resistance, the growth of the Ku Klux Klan, and the arch-segregationist voice of the new media king in Albany, James H. Gray, who controlled the major daily newspaper, a radio station, and the local television station, made for a formidable Jim Crow alliance.

Albany attorney B.C. Gardner sent *Herald* clippings to the chancellor and that fall the Board of Regents declined to renew the college president's annual contract.

The same year that Aaron Brown was fired, a new and powerful voice took up the civil rights cause in

The "Colored Entrance" sign for the long-closed Albany Theater remained in place over the alley next to the theater on Jackson Street until it was donated in the early 1990s to the Albany Civil Rights Institute where it is on display. Todd Stone Photography

local television station, made for a formidable Jim Crow alliance. Yet there were glimmers of hope. C.B. King's eloquent voice was heard in the white man's courtrooms around southwest Georgia. In 1957, some Criterion Club members petitioned the Albany city commission for improvements in the Lincoln Heights neighborhood infrastructure. By 1958, within 10 years of its establishment, the local Voters League could point with pride to the registration of nearly a fifth of those blacks in Albany eligible to vote. There was even a spark of hope in what later civil rights workers would call Terrible Terrell. D.U. Pullum asked Korean War veteran Lucius Holloway to serve with him as vice president of the Terrell County branch of the NAACP. Holloway agreed and together they recruited members. And in 1959, looking ahead to the important role that students would play in the movement, black businessman Thomas Chatmon, Sr. organized a local NAACP Youth Council in Albany.

SNCC worker Cordell Reagon accompanied Charles Sherrod to southwest Georgia in October 1961. Danny Lyon/Magnum Photos

5

The story of the Albany Movement is often told in King-centric terms as a tale of failure—i.e., it took off in December 1961 when Martin Luther King, Jr., came to Albany, and ended in the summer of 1962 when King left the city as segregated as when he had first come. According to this historical version, the movement was significant nationally, in that King learned from his mistakes in Albany and went on to success the next year in Birmingham. The reality, however, is that the Albany Movement of 1961-1962 was the most well-known chapter of a centuries-long freedom struggle in southwest Georgia. Its roots go back to runaway slaves, black Reconstruction politicians, and the work of C.W. King, Aaron Brown, and other African American leaders who founded the local NAACP branch, the Voters League, the

reserved for whites, at Albany's Arctic Bear drive-in restaurant. When a white patron complained and the manager asked the three young women to leave, they refused. Jones would go on to become a student protest leader at ASC. ASC students on campus continued to be harassed by the age-old practice of white men speeding through the college campus, tossing out racial epithets, bottles, and even bags of urine and rotten garbage. On several occasions white men were found wandering the corridors of McIntosh Hall, a women's dormitory. Students were unhappy with campus security's failure to prevent such incursions and they demanded that locks be installed on dormitory doors.

In the winter of 1960, a number of ASC students were inspired by the student sit-ins that began in Greensboro, NC, in February and spread to 125 cities

ASC, SNCC AND THE ALBANY MOVEMENT, 1959-1961

Criterion Club, and other organizations that challenged Jim Crow oppression. And the movement continued long after King departed Albany right up to the present. The Albany Movement, then, was a local movement which invited the participation of Martin Luther King, Jr., and thus received national attention and support.

Another oft-told version of the Albany Movement's history has its student activism commencing with the arrival of two Student Nonviolent Coordinating Committee (SNCC, pronounced "Snick") workers Charles Sherrod and Cordell Reagon. In fact, student activism began during Aaron Brown's presidency at ASC when he encouraged faculty and students to join the NAACP. It continued after Brown was fired, with the establishment of the local NAACP Youth Council in 1959 and the collective actions of ASC students. One of the first student sit-ins took place in fall 1959, when a NAACP Youth Council member Annette Jones and two fellow ASC students decided to eat at the outdoor tables,

within two months and led to the founding of SNCC in April. When ASC students elected Student Government Association (SGA) leadership in May, they chose individuals who would play a key role in leading student protests in the next academic year. That same month, the Georgia Board of Regents addressed the student sit-in movement by adopting a new policy that any University System student (ASC was part of the University System of Georgia) accused of or indicted for breaking a state or federal law, such as disturbing the peace, was to be suspended until s/he was convicted or found innocent. Thus as ASC students inclined to greater activism, their conservative college president William H. Dennis, who had succeeded Aaron Brown, was handed the tools necessary to quell student protests.

When he hired Irene Asbury in 1960 as the new Dean of Students, President Dennis was probably unaware of her sympathies for the civil rights movement.

African American osteopath William G. Anderson, center, was elected president of the Albany Movement at its founding on November 17, 1961. AE Jenkins Photography

In the summer she conducted a workshop for the new SGA leadership, empowering them for the coming year's challenges. In November 1960, SGA President Leviticus Roberts and other SGA leaders went to Atlanta to meet with SNCC leaders Julian Bond and John Lewis and other black college SGA presidents to discuss their role in the movement.

In December 1960, attention shifted from the students to community leaders when four members of the Criterion Club were allowed to meet with the Albany city commission for 30 minutes to discuss voting and other matters. The commission appointed African American osteopath Dr. William G. Anderson and President Dennis to a "special subcommittee on minority group housing" to deal with the Criterion Club's concerns raised in 1957 about the Lincoln Heights infrastructure. When a group of African American ministers, however, raised concerns in the new year about the city's racial climate and asked the city commission to investigate acts of violence against a minister's house and on ASC students, faculty, and property, the commissioners refused to respond.

During the same month—January 1961—Charlayne Hunter and Hamilton Holmes integrated the University of Georgia. In Albany, WALB-AM radio station, recently sold

by media mogul James H. Gray, lambasted the integration of the state's flagship campus, complaining that UGA's *Who's Who* would become *Who Dat*. Six ASC student leaders, including SGA President Leviticus Roberts and Annette Jones, wrote a letter to the *Albany Herald* under the pseudonym Leonard Carson, protesting the inferior conditions of segregation and demanding equality. In reaction to a barrage of phone calls and verbal attacks, President Dennis informed the press and a student assembly on campus the day after the *Herald* published the Leonard Carson letter that there was no Leonard Carson at ASC. At that point student leader and NAACP Youth Council secretary Bernice Johnson stood up and bravely declared, "There are five hundred Leonard Carsons here," and the students cheered.

ASC students and their college president were at loggerheads and matters deteriorated. SGA members met with Dennis to present a list of their concerns. His response was to tell an assembly of students they were not to participate in civil rights activities and that ASC did not approve of the sit-in movement. In February, Dennis suspended the SGA and padlocked its offices. When Dean Asbury could not secure a meeting with the president to discuss students' concerns and the college's treatment of them, she resigned, married Air Force Lieutenant Vic Wright stationed at Turner Field, and put her energies into the movement as it took off later in the fall of 1961.

The summer of 1961 saw several new players in the unfolding drama of the southwest Georgia civil rights struggle. On the ASC campus President Dennis replaced Irene Asbury with Charles W. Minor as the new Dean of Students. Unlike his predecessor, Minor had no sympathy for student protestors. Meanwhile, ASC student protestors found new off-campus leadership with the arrival of two SNCC workers in Albany—Charles Sherrod and Cordell Reagon. The lean, soft-spoken, 24-year-old Sherrod was the leader of SNCC's new voter registration effort in southwest Georgia. A graduate of Virginia Union College and a minister, Sherrod had joined SNCC in 1960 and had been arrested and jailed in South Carolina and Mississippi. Sherrod's initial plan was to start a voter registration drive in Terrell County, but he quickly learned how terrified African Americans were in Terrible

different from the NAACP's strategies. They won over a number of Youth Council members, much to the chagrin of Thomas Chatmon, the council's founder and adult advisor. Already the lines of division in the African American community were becoming visible—students vs. community leaders and SNCC vs. NAACP.

Divisions in the black community would continue to plague civil rights efforts throughout 1961 and 1962. Yet at important moments, Albany's African Americans rose above the divisions. A lack of unity, however, was not a problem for Albany whites. More so than many other southern white communities, Albany whites remained strongly unified in their defense of segregation. At the helm in this struggle to protect white supremacy was the city's police chief, Laurie Pritchett. Unlike the stereotypical southern law enforcement officer, Pritchett usually did not resort to violence in confronting nonviolent demonstrators. Anticipating an eventual nonviolent assault on Jim Crow in Albany, he trained his

One of the first student sit-ins took place in fall 1959, when a NAACP Youth Council member Annette Jones and two fellow ASC students decided to eat at the outdoor tables, reserved for whites, at Albany's Arctic Bear drive-in restaurant.

Terrell and could find few who were willing to go to the courthouse to register. So he changed course, and with 18-year-old Reagon, a Freedom Rider who had been jailed in Mississippi's dreaded Parchman Penitentiary, came to Albany in October 1961.

C.W. King let the two SNCC workers stay in one of his buildings in Albany and they got right to work. They would shoot hoops with high school students on the local school playgrounds and talk with them about freedom, the Freedom Rides, and the student sit-ins. They also visited the ASC campus and met student activists Annette Jones and Bernice Johnson. Word spread and Sherrod met with local minister Horace C. Boyd of Shiloh Baptist Church. Soon the SNCC leaders were holding meetings with students at Shiloh. They held workshops on nonviolent tactics and taught freedom songs to the students and adults who attended. Sherrod and Reagon met members of the NAACP Youth Council and explained how SNCC tactics of nonviolent direct action and going to jail without accepting bail were

police force in the use of nonviolent tactics. He also relied on African American informants to keep him apprised of demonstration plans by activists.

On November 1, 1961, the Interstate Commerce Commission (ICC) ruling requiring the desegregation of interstate transportation facilities went into effect and Sherrod and Reagon wanted to test the ruling at the Trailways Bus Station in Albany. Chatmon and Sherrod agreed that NAACP Youth Council students would undertake the test on November 1, but not in the name of the NAACP. Word of the bus station test leaked out and on October 30 Chief Pritchett warned the city commission to expect demonstrations soon.

In addition to the students testing the desegregation of the bus station facilities, Sherrod and Reagon, along with white SNCC observer Salynn McCollum, planned to ride the bus from Atlanta to Albany to test it as riders. Their Freedom Ride, however, was a bust. No students were there when they alighted from the bus and entered the white waiting room. Disappointed, they left and

Evelyn Toney, Julian Carswell, and Eddie Wilson, the first students arrested at the Trailways Bus Station on November 22, 1961, were bailed out and given a meal by local NAACP President Dr. E.D. Hamilton and NAACP Youth Council Advisor Thomas Chatmon, Sr. The Thomas C. Chatmon, Sr. Family Collection

eventually persuaded nine students to go to the station and enter the white waiting room. When the police ordered them out, they left and no arrests were made.

The courage of the nine students to challenge the now illegal color line at the interstate bus station put pressure on community leaders to get more involved in what was clearly becoming a growing student movement in Albany. On November 17, leaders of SNCC, the NAACP Youth

Five days later, on November 22, the day before Thanksgiving, three members of the NAACP Youth Council—high schoolers Julian Carswell and Eddie Wilson and ASC student Evelyn Toney—were arrested for attempting to desegregate the Trailways Bus Station. They were jailed but were bonded out in a few hours. Later that day ASC dismissed its students for the holiday and many of them headed for the Trailways station along with Dean Minor

At the helm in this struggle to protect white supremacy was the city's police chief, Laurie Pritchett. Unlike the stereotypical southern law enforcement officer, Pritchett usually did not resort to violence in confronting nonviolent demonstrators.

Council, the NAACP, the Criterion Club, the Voters League, the Federated Women's Club, the Ministerial Alliance, and the Lincoln Heights Improvement Association met at the home of real estate broker Slater King, brother of C.B. King, and created a formal organization they named The Albany Movement. Osteopath William G. Anderson was chosen president, Slater King first vice president, Irene Asbury Wright second vice president, and C.B. King legal counsel.

who was determined that none of his charges cross the color line. Despite the dean's best efforts, two ASC students and SNCC supporters—Bertha Gober of Atlanta and Blanton Hall of Athens—managed to get into the white waiting room where Laurie Pritchett and his men were waiting. The police chief had them arrested and jailed. Unlike the NAACP Youth Council students, Gober and Hall chose to remain in jail over Thanksgiving, generating sympathy and raising concern in Albany's African American community.

The newly organized Albany Movement called for its first mass meeting the Saturday after Thanksgiving. The meeting's location—Mt. Zion Baptist Church, across the street from H.C. Boyd's Shiloh Baptist Church—was significant as Mt. Zion was the church of Albany's African American elite, its professional class, including college professors and ASC President William H. Dennis. When Pastor E. James Grant opened Mt. Zion's doors, he signaled that the movement was no longer just a student affair, but a cause endorsed by the entire black community. Today the Old Mt. Zion Church building is a key element of the Albany Civil Rights Institute complex.

Reverend Grant risked not only the opposition of some of his members but also his daytime job as principal of a school in Baker County. Bad Baker, as SNCC members called it, had changed little from the days of Sheriff Claude Screws. Screws's successor was one of his deputies, L. Warren "Gator" Johnson, an apt pupil of the brutal sheriff. Five months before the mass

arrested students. Bertha Gober and Blanton Hall had been released from jail that morning, but not before receiving notice from ASC of their suspension for being arrested. All five of the students spoke of their actions and their jail experiences. Freedom songs and spirituals punctuated the meeting and singing soon became one of the hallmarks of the southwest Georgia movement (see Chapter 10).

The following night, Annette Jones, Bernice Johnson, Evelyn Toney and a half dozen other student activists visited ASC students in their dorms, drumming up support for a protest march the next day. Monday morning, Jones and Johnson led the first mass march in Albany from the ASC campus, across the Flint River to City Hall where the five arrested students were on trial. Over 500 college and high school students and adults demonstrated as the five students were speedily tried, convicted, fined, and released. Joining Sherrod and Reagon was their SNCC colleague Charles Jones who led

Jones and Johnson led the first mass march in Albany from the ASC campus, across the Flint River to City Hall where the five arrested students were on trial. Over 500 college and high school students and adults demonstrated as the five students were speedily tried, convicted, fined, and released.

meeting at Mt. Zion, Gator Johnson arrested Charlie Ware, an African American field hand at Coca Cola magnate Robert Woodruff's Ichuaway plantation in Baker County, for public drunkenness at Woodruff's annual Fourth of July barbecue. Apparently, Ware had flirted with the African American mistress of the plantation's white overseer who complained to Gator Johnson. The sheriff arrested Ware at his home late that night, beat and handcuffed him, and drove him to the Baker County jail. There, in his cruiser, Gator put a penknife in Ware's bound hands and radioed state troopers saying, "There's a nigger coming at me with a knife and I'll have to shoot him!" The sheriff then shot Ware twice in the neck and once in the shoulder. Miraculously, Ware survived and was indicted by a Baker County grand jury for assaulting the sheriff.

Charlie Ware was languishing in the Baker County jail as the Albany Movement mass meeting got underway at Mt. Zion. The stars of the gathering were the five

the singing protestors in prayer. Chief Pritchett and his men were there but refrained from making any arrests.

ASC student protest leaders had witnessed the first and last mass protest actions of ASC students that Monday, November 27, 1961. The next day college officials began taking severe steps to curtail student protest. Students with campus jobs lost them. Threats of dismissal and losing financial aid frightened many students from supporting movement activities. When Charles Sherrod visited the campus on Tuesday, President Dennis had him arrested for trespassing. While Dennis was curbing the enthusiasm for protest on campus, the willingness of the larger African American community in town to take direct action in challenging Jim Crow was growing. All that was needed was a spark or two to turn the smoldering protest movement into a conflagration. The next month—December 1961—Freedom Riders and Martin Luther King, Jr., would provide those sparks.

Students pray in protest at City Hall, Albany, December 1961. AE Jenkins Photography

6

The highpoint of the 1961-1962 Albany Movement was the nine days in December 1961 that featured the arrest and eventual release of 750 people, including eight Freedom Riders, most of the Albany Movement leadership, and Martin Luther King, Jr. In the first days of December, SNCC workers in Albany—Charles Sherrod, Cordell Reagon and Charles Jones—encouraged SNCC Executive Secretary James Forman to organize a Freedom Ride from Atlanta to Albany to test the Albany Union train station's compliance with the ICC ruling requiring desegregated interstate travel facilities. Jones and Forman put together a group of eight Freedom Riders (four African American and four white) to depart Atlanta on Sunday, December 10. For the African American riders, Forman chose himself, SNCC office manager Norma

bystanders, including Charles Jones and ASC student Bertha Gober. The 11 arrestees were taken to City Hall where they were booked for disorderly conduct and obstructing traffic and incarcerated in the city jail. In the meantime, the crowd that had come to greet them marched to Shiloh Baptist Church where others joined them for an emotional mass meeting. The testifying, praying, and singing assisted African Americans in Albany as they girded themselves for what was to come.

Monday morning, December 11, Marion King, Slater King's wife, and a small group of people gathered at City Hall to pray for justice for the Freedom Riders jailed inside. City police arrested and jailed King and her companions on the same charges as the Freedom Riders. African Americans in Albany were outraged that first the

NINE DAYS IN DECEMBER,
1961

Collins, Southern Christian Leadership Conference (SCLC) staffer Bernard Lee, and Atlanta University graduate student Lenora Taitt. The four whites who volunteered were SNCC Field Secretary Bob Zellner, Danish journalist Per Laursen, former student and SNCC activist Joan Browning, and SNCC and Students for a Democratic Society (SDS) activist Tom Hayden. A ninth person—Hayden's new wife Casey Hayden, another SNCC and SDS activist—accompanied the Freedom Riders as a designated observer.

On Sunday, the eight Freedom Riders and observer boarded the train in Atlanta and proceeded to Albany, arriving at Union Station, location today of Thronateeska Heritage Center. They walked into the white waiting room and then outside where a crowd of Albany Movement supporters greeted them. The welcoming cheers agitated Police Chief Laurie Pritchett who lost his temper and arrested the eight Freedom Riders and three

youthful outsiders of the Freedom Ride were arrested and then a respectable middle class professional like Marion King, a physical therapist, was thrown in jail as well. Even conservative African Americans were moved to attend the mass meeting that night at Shiloh. The Freedom Riders were bailed out that afternoon and they came to the mass meeting which was so large it spilled over to Mt. Zion Baptist Church across the street. Plans were made to march in protest to City Hall the next day when the Freedom Riders' trials were to start. Charles Sherrod met with a group of his most reliable high school students encouraging them to join Tuesday's march and help fill up the jails. He knew that when Albany officials ran out of jail space, they would be forced to deal with the Albany Movement's demands that the city abide by the ICC desegregation ruling at its bus and train stations and that it enter into a discussion with black leaders about desegregating the city.

Students and movement activists Rev. William Boyd, Irene Asbury Wright, and Slater King kneel in protest, Albany, December 1961.
AE Jenkins Photography

A steady rain on Tuesday morning, December 12, did not dampen the spirits of the 400 African Americans—many of them high school and college students—as they lined up at Shiloh behind Sherrod and walked three abreast down Whitney Avenue to the end of the block. There they turned north on Jackson Street and headed downtown to City Hall where the first of the Freedom Riders' trials—that of Per Laursen—was starting. Arriving at City Hall about 10 a.m., they began to walk around the large block on which City Hall was located, singing and chanting freedom songs. As they walked in front of City Hall, they passed by the city's festive Christmas decorations hanging across Pine Avenue, a rain-soaked reminder that this year December would be remembered for its mass meetings, marches, and jailings, rather than holiday parties and the exchange of gifts.

By the time they began a third circuit of the block, Chief Pritchett ordered the arrest of the 267 people still marching and herded them into an alley behind the city jail where they waited in the drenching rain to be booked. At the mass meeting at Shiloh that night, people came to church to sing, pray, and listen to their movement leaders encourage them to continue to challenge the oppressive white power structure. While Shiloh rang with preaching, prayers and freedom songs, Albany Police Chief Laurie Pritchett was busy contracting with the sheriffs of surrounding counties to rent jail space. He was determined to have plenty of prison space for the protestors the movement offered up for arrest. His rental of jail cells in Bad Baker, Terrible Terrell, Lee, Mitchell, Worth, and Sumter counties was more than a logistical solution to his problem. It also terrorized African Americans who were very familiar with the reputations of these counties and their respective sheriffs. Everyone knew that Baker County Sheriff Gator Johnson had shot the handcuffed Charlie Ware just outside the county jail in Newton the previous summer. And they soon would learn that Terrell County Sheriff Z.T. Zeke Mathews slapped Charles Sherrod "a couple of times" and cut his lip when the SNCC leader was transferred to the county jail in Dawson.

Early Wednesday morning, December 13, frightened prisoners boarded buses in Albany to be transported to the outlying counties. A 15-year-old girl was sent by bus to Camilla where the Mitchell County sheriff reminded the new arrivals, "You're not in Albany any more." She and 53 other girls were squeezed into a six-bed cell with "no mattresses, just steel beds." The food was disgusting— "Dinner was a big spoonful of raw black-eyed peas, bread and raw fat-back." Meanwhile, on another bus heading to Newton, were Annette Jones, Marion King, 73-year-old Mary Williams, and 36 other women. The Baker County jail food was as inedible as that in Camilla—breakfast was "grits topped with grease and a generous portion of pork belly complete with nipples." Some prisoners went days without eating. The Lee County Stockade, formerly home to the county's chain gang, was the destination of another 51 women arrested in Albany—"there was no place to sleep, just wet and dirty mattresses in the cell." A great fear of many of the transported prisoners was that no one knew where they were. And, as Albany Movement President Dr. William G. Anderson recalled years later,

national and even international media attention and more reporters witnessed Wednesday's arrests. Chief Pritchett explained to the newsmen, "We can't tolerate the N.A.A.C.P. or the Student Nonviolent Committee or any other 'nigger' organization to take over the town with mass demonstrations."

Whites in Albany were not the only ones concerned about the NAACP and SNCC coming and taking over. Some of the Albany Movement members feared loss of control of their own local movement to national civil rights groups. SNCC leaders had clearly shown their ability to inspire and lead local high school and college students. Meanwhile, NAACP Southeast Regional Director Ruby Hurley and NAACP Georgia Field Secretary Vernon Jordan were doing their best to co-opt Dr. Anderson and bring the Albany Movement under NAACP control. As the idea of calling in Dr. Martin Luther King, Jr. was floated by Albany Movement leaders, some objected for fear that King's organization, the

As they walked in front of City Hall, [the protesters] passed by the city's festive Christmas decorations hanging across Pine Avenue, a rain-soaked reminder that this year December would be remembered for its mass meetings, marches, and jailings, rather than holiday parties and the exchange of gifts.

people feared going to jail in southwest Georgia because they knew individuals who had gone to jail and had never been heard of again.

The morning that prisoners began being bused to neighboring counties, Albany Movement Vice President Slater King led 75 others to kneel in prayer outside City Hall as the trial of Freedom Rider Per Laursen resumed. Chief Pritchett arrested only King and brought him inside to the judge who sentenced him to five days in jail. When word of Slater King's fate reached people meeting at Shiloh, they organized another mass march. Cordell Reagon got word out to sympathetic teachers who discreetly let students go to Shiloh. Eventually 300 headed downtown, circled the City Hall block and returned to Shiloh where they regrouped and returned downtown. This time, Chief Pritchett, pressured by an angry city commission, arrested the 202 protestors. The Albany demonstrations and arrests received significant

Southern Christian Leadership Council (SCLC), would try to take charge. Further complicating matters was the rivalry among the national civil rights organizations themselves. SNCC members derisively referred to Dr. King as "De Lawd" who flew into a community with the SCLC and the press in tow, preached, marched, and moved on. SNCC, on the other hand, moved in and became part of the community. Both SNCC and SCLC had problems with the NAACP which was not enthusiastic about King's and SNCC's direct action tactics, preferring to dismantle segregation through the courts.

The Albany Movement leadership finally agreed to invite Dr. King. Dr. Anderson had already contacted King's lieutenant, Ralph Abernathy, who discussed the matter with King. King and Anderson then talked and King agreed to come. Meanwhile the mass meetings and protests continued. After the 202 demonstrators were arrested on Wednesday, bringing the total arrested that week to over 480, more than 700 African Americans jammed into Shiloh to hear more calls for protest and to be fortified with prayer and song. In addition to promoting prayer vigils at City Hall and mass marches downtown, speakers called for a boycott of a dozen white-owned stores in downtown Albany. At the next evening's mass meeting, Albany Movement Executive Secretary Marion Page reported that the boycott was already working and the businesses were feeling the pinch.

In the meantime, a small biracial negotiating committee was formed to handle negotiations between the Albany Movement and Mayor Asa Kelley and the city commissioners; some progress was made but on key points the city was intransigent. On Friday, December 15, the Albany Movement proposed to the city that in return for a permanent end to protest demonstrations, the city would completely desegregate the bus and train stations in 30 days, allow the substitution of property bonds for cash bonds for those still in jail, and create a biracial committee to discuss

segregation in the city. Not hopeful that the city would agree, some movement leaders feared the movement was faltering. Dr. Anderson called Dr. King stressing the importance of his coming to Albany that night to reenergize the African American community.

King, Abernathy, and SCLC Executive Director Wyatt Tee Walker drove down from Atlanta Friday afternoon. Word spread that Dr. King would speak at Shiloh and the church quickly filled to the rafters as did Mt. Zion across the street. Also speaking that evening was Ruby Hurley who put in a plug for the boycott—"When those cash registers are not ringing they understand what you're talking about." But the people came to hear and be inspired by Martin Luther King, Jr., and he did not disappoint. According to Dr. Anderson and others, King was inspired by the power of the foot-stomping a cappella southwest Georgia black Baptist hymns, freedom songs, and chants shouted by the 1,500 voices in the two jam-packed sanctuaries. When King finished at Shiloh,

As Albany Movement President Dr. William G. Anderson recalled years later, people feared going to jail in southwest Georgia because they knew individuals who had gone to jail and had never been heard of again.

Albany Movement First Vice President Slater King and Second Vice President Irene Asbury Wright lead protestors on march to City Hall, Albany, December 1961. AE Jenkins Photography

Anderson persuaded him to walk across the street and speak to the people in Mt. Zion. When the exhausted King concluded his remarks, Anderson informed him that the people he spoke to at Shiloh had left and the church refilled with those who could not get into the sanctuary earlier; they crossed back across the street and King spoke again. During the evening Anderson invited King to join their protest march the next day. King agreed.

The march on Saturday, December 16, was contingent on the city's response to the movement's latest proposal. When Mayor Kelley rejected it Saturday morning, preparations for the march began. It was late afternoon when King and Anderson led 265 others walking double-file towards City Hall. Chief Pritchett arrested all 267 marchers, bringing the total for the week to 749. As before, protestors were booked and then bused to jails in the outlying counties. King, Abernathy, and Anderson were driven to Americus for safekeeping in the Sumter County jail. While King and Anderson spent two nights in the care of Sheriff Fred Chappell (King called him the "meanest man in the world"), the rivalry between SCLC, SNCC, and the Albany Movement boiled over in public. Abernathy (bailed out of jail) and Walker were busy in Atlanta and Albany fundraising for the Albany Movement and having the money sent to SCLC, rather than the local movement. In addition, while SCLC looked ahead to a mass protest campaign centered on King spending Christmas in jail, Albany Movement leaders were looking for a way to reopen negotiations with the city. Albany Movement Executive Secretary

city refused to put the agreement in a written form that both parties could sign. With some misgivings, King agreed to the proposal and bailed out of jail.

Monday evening before flying back to Atlanta, King spoke to an overflow crowd at Shiloh where he emphasized the positive aspects of the city's concessions. Marion Page, talking to the same group, called the concessions a "first step." Meanwhile, city officials denied that any concessions had been made. Mayor Kelley reported that U.S. Attorney General Robert F. Kennedy had congratulated the city on resolving the dispute without resorting to violence. City leaders showed their appreciation to white newsmen for their coverage of the city's struggle with the movement by treating them to a steak dinner at the segregated Radium Springs Country Club.

Within days of the settlement, four days before Christmas, Marion Page announced the resumption of the boycott of white merchants downtown. City officials

The holidays were especially bleak for the 40 ASC students who had been arrested or heavily involved in the movement. The coal in their stocking was a suspension notice from the college.

Marion Page made it clear at a Sunday press conference that neither SCLC nor any other national organization had taken over the local movement.

Monday morning, December 18, King and Anderson were brought to Albany for trial on the charges of parading without a permit and obstructing traffic the previous Saturday. Before the trial could begin, it was recessed as negotiations had resumed between the city and the Albany Movement. City officials were now eager to have King out of jail and out of town and to end the threat of future mass protests and the economic boycott of white merchants, and thus were willing to make concessions. According to the agreement reached, the city would: desegregate the bus and rail stations; release all prisoners who owned property or were employed on security bonds; and allow the Albany Movement "to present its demands for other changes in racial customs" at the January 11 meeting of the city commission. Despite the efforts of the Albany Movement leaders, the

had reneged on the part of the agreement that allowed prisoners who had put up $200 cash bonds "to get their money back and post property bonds." To do their Christmas shopping, many African Americans drove to Moultrie and other nearby towns. Discouraged that whites were already reneging on the agreement that ended the December protests, a number of movement participants refused to put up traditional Yuletide decorations and had what they called a Black Christmas. The holidays were especially bleak for the 40 ASC students who had been arrested or heavily involved in the movement. The coal in their stocking was a suspension notice from the college. As they reflected on 1961, African Americans in southwest Georgia could take great pride in the blows they had struck against Jim Crow. But it was clear that Jim Crow was still very much alive, and as they looked ahead to 1962, they knew the struggle for freedom would continue to demand much of them.

Folk singer Guy Carawan and Bernice Johnson and several of her fellow students suspended from ASC chat with Martin Luther King, Jr. at the SCLC Citizenship School Training Center, Dorchester, Georgia, January 1962. Seated to the right of Johnson are Carolyn Toney, Brenda Darden, Evelyn Toney, Eddie Burnett, Charles Ransom, and Bobby Burch. Bobby Burch Collection

7

For many people the Albany Movement consisted of two discrete periods (November-December 1961 and July-August 1962) which featured mass arrests and the presence of Dr. Martin Luther King, Jr. Lost in this conception is the critical six months linking these two periods. The developments in the first half of 1962 illustrate how the Albany Movement was more than just two famous highpoints involving King, but rather part and parcel of the long 200-year freedom struggle in southwest Georgia.

Albany State College students who marched in protest and got arrested did so at great risk. When the college followed through on its threat to suspend them, at least six of the most active leaders—Annette Jones, James Jones, Bernice Johnson, Bertha Gober, Blanton

students tried to get library cards at the all-white Carnegie Public Library. They were denied and left before they were arrested. Another small group attempted to get served at the Trailways Bus Station lunch counter. They, too, left before getting arrested. At the same time in early January, a number of students met at Shiloh Baptist Church with new Southern Christian Leadership Conference (SCLC) staffers Dorothy Cotton and Andrew Young. Young had recently become director of Septima Clark's citizenship schools program. Clark had established the schools in coastal South Carolina and Georgia in the late 1950s to teach basic reading skills to poor African Americans so they could pass the literacy tests required for voter registration. SCLC took over the program in 1961 and

WINTER AND SPRING ACTION,
1962

Hall, and Anne Booyer—were expelled. While ASC Dean Charles Minor and President William Dennis presided at kangaroo court suspension hearings in early January, former dean and activist Irene Asbury Wright and other concerned adults used their influence to help get some of the expelled students accepted into private historically black colleges like Spelman, Morehouse, and Morris Brown in Atlanta. African American community pressure on President Dennis led him to write some of the suspended students in mid-January that they might be considered for readmission in mid-March for the spring quarter. Some suspended students applied for readmission, were accepted, and graduated on time. Some of the suspended students never returned to college at all, and several of the young men were drafted and ended up serving in Vietnam.

Many of the suspended students continued their involvement with the movement. Several small groups of

set up a training center for citizenship school teachers at an old freedmen's school in Dorchester, near Savannah. At Dorchester, black community leaders from around the South attended weeklong workshops, learning basic civics, African American history, how to teach literacy, and how to set up the citizenship schools in their own communities.

At Shiloh, Cotton and Young recruited for Dorchester a dozen or more students suspended by ASC. Andrew Young later recalled that the training session for the Albany students "was the liveliest week we ever had." With song leaders Bernice Johnson and Rutha Harris, the music that had become so identified with the Albany Movement became an integral part of the workshop that week. And after the singing, came dancing. The African American history lectures by SCLC staffer Jack O'Dell were based on W.E.B. Du Bois's *The Souls of Black Folk*. Du Bois's essays on

Bobby Burch's Certificate of Attendance for participating in the Citizenship School Training Program at Dorchester, January 1962, signed by Septima Clark, Dorothy Cotton, Andrew Young, Ralph Abernathy, Martin Luther King, Jr., and Guy Carawan. Bobby Burch Collection

Dougherty County resonated with the Albany students. O'Dell showed how the current movement was historically part of a much longer freedom struggle that went back to Reconstruction. According to Young, the idea that the modern civil rights movement "had the potential to be a Second Reconstruction emerged in this workshop."

The Albany students returned to their community invigorated and enthusiastic about setting up citizenship schools in local churches. Before she went off to Spelman College, Annette Jones started a citizenship school at C.K. Smith Presbyterian Church, a small church that was supportive of the movement. When Andrew Young returned to Albany for Dr. King's trial at the end of February, he took the opportunity to teach a citizenship class at Trinity Baptist Church.

It was clear that the December protests and mass arrests had inspired the students to continue the struggle in Albany into the new year by attempting to desegregate white institutions and setting up citizenship schools to increase voter registration. SNCC leaders were daily models to young African Americans challenging Jim Crow. Sherrod, Reagon, and Charles Jones accompanied them to Dorchester. Sherrod and Jones sat-in at the Trailways Bus Station lunch counter when Albany police arrested them for "loitering." Going to jail was no longer a shame for these young people, but a badge of honor. The impact of this change in attitude was not limited to Albany. Word of these many assaults on Jim Crow circulated in the outlying plantation counties like Terrible Terrell and Lee. Sherrod had been planning a strategy for carrying the movement beyond Albany to rural southwest Georgia, but students at African American high schools in Terrell and Lee counties launched school boycotts and beat him to the punch. In both cases the boycotts were reactions to the expulsion of students. On January 17, Charles Wingfield was expelled from the Lee County Training School (LCTS) for requesting better school equipment. The next day beautician Carolyn Daniels's son Roychester Patterson was expelled from Carver High School in Dawson for discussing civil rights at lunchtime. On January 19, 90 percent of LCTS students refused to attend classes. The following week, however, white supremacists quashed both boycotts, refused to reinstate the expelled students, and prohibited SNCC members from the school grounds. Sherrod soon befriended Roy Patterson and his mother and they became stalwarts of the Terrell County movement.

Meanwhile, in Albany it was a suspended college student who aroused the ire of white supremacists. Ola Mae Quarterman was an 18-year-old freshman at ASC when she was arrested for protesting in December and received her suspension notice. On Friday, January 12,

American taxis. Since blacks comprised 80 percent of its passengers, Cities Transit soon felt the pinch of running nearly empty buses. Ten days after her arrest, Quarterman was tried, convicted, fined $100, and sentenced to a month in jail, 25 days of which were suspended.

The day after Quarterman's trial, the Albany city commission finally allowed Albany Movement President William Anderson and Executive Secretary Marion Page to make a presentation requesting the establishment of a biracial committee to discuss segregation. But before any discussion of their proposal could take place, Mayor Asa Kelley adjourned the meeting saying the commission would get back to them within 10 days.

The last week of January, Albany Movement representatives met with Cities Transit officials and offered to end the boycott, now 90 percent effective, if the bus company would agree in writing to desegregate the buses and begin hiring black drivers. The company

"I paid my damn 20 cents . . . and I can sit where I want." Years later Quarterman recalled, "Then he stuck his finger in my face. . . . I said, 'Get your damn finger out of my face.'"

Quarterman boarded the bus in east Albany to go to a SNCC voter registration meeting. After paying her 20 cent fare and before she could take her seat, the driver, as often happens, accelerated thus jolting the new passenger into the closest seat at the front of the bus. When she decided to remain there, the driver confronted her ordering her to a back seat. "I paid my damn 20 cents," she retorted, "and I can sit where I want." Years later Quarterman recalled, "Then he stuck his finger in my face. . . . I said, 'Get your damn finger out of my face.' Just like that." The infuriated driver found a policeman who arrested the young woman for using vulgarity. In response, the Albany Movement expanded its boycott of downtown stores to include Cities Transit, Inc., which ran the city buses. SNCC leader Charles Jones, meanwhile, helped organize a car pool and observers noticed a boom in the use of African

was willing to do both to avoid going out of business, but first it had to get assurances from the city commission that the city would not enforce the local segregation ordinances on the buses. At its January 31 meeting, the arch-segregationist majority, led by Ford automobile dealer C.B. "Bunny" Pritchett, Jr. (no relation to the police chief), voted to enforce city bus segregation, thus forcing the company to shut down. Earlier that day, the commission had stated that the city had made no concessions to the Albany Movement in December, including the establishment of a biracial committee.

Two nights after the city commission vote, the Albany Movement responded at a mass meeting at Bethel A.M.E. Church with a call for a "full-scale boycott" of downtown merchants. Movement leaders expanded their goals to include desegregation of parks and libraries as well as equal employment opportunity.

In the meantime, fissures became visible in the white community as moderate businessmen and Mayor Asa Kelley questioned the wisdom of the arch-segregationist city commission's vote on January 31. Merchants, hurt by the black consumer boycott, agreed with the Chamber of Commerce that bus service must be reestablished. In mid-February, the bus company resumed service on its mostly white routes. On March 2, Cities Transit hired its first African American driver in an effort to meet one of the movement's demands. But the buses remained segregated and the boycott continued. The following week, Cities Transit shut down again, but this time Albany would go for three years without a public bus system.

The end of February and end of March saw the first trials to come out of the December protests. Dr. King returned to Albany for his trial on February 27. In Judge A.N. Durden's Recorder's Court, King faced charges of parading without a permit on December 16.

him to the rear or colored section. The Haydens, Zellner and Laursen got up and sat with Sherrod in the rear. Deputies then jumped on the four whites and pulled them out of the room. Casey Hayden, wearing her white gloves, "hooked my legs under the bench so that they had to pry me out sideways" dragging her "across a row of seats and into the hall." Judge Crow watched this violent enforcement of segregation from the bench, and told reporters that "the officers were enforcing a rule of the court."

In mid-March, Albany Movement leaders strengthened their boycott efforts by establishing "vigilante committees" that would identify African Americans shopping at boycotted stores. Dr. Anderson, Slater King, and a couple of other movement leaders set up a picket line to promote the boycott and soon found themselves arrested and jailed. While the Albany Movement adults were getting arrested for picketing, SNCC leaders Reagon and Jones were harnessing the power of high schoolers

Charles Sherrod entered the courtroom and walked to the front section to sit with the Freedom Riders when Chief Deputy Lamar Stewart knocked him to the floor and dragged him to the rear or colored section.

After Chief Pritchett's testimony, Durden recessed the trial, indicating it could be two months before he handed down his decision.

A month after King's trial came the Freedom Riders' trials. In December, Municipal Court Judge Abner Israel, who presided over the first Freedom Rider trial, bound over the eight Freedom Riders and three bystanders arrested December 10 for trial in Dougherty Superior Court on state charges of unlawful assembly. On Monday morning, March 26, the three white male Freedom Riders—Per Laursen, Bob Zellner, and Tom Hayden—and Tom's wife, Casey Hayden, the designated observer for the Freedom Ride, sat in the white section of Superior Court Judge Carl E. Crow's segregated courtroom filled with 100 spectators. Charles Sherrod entered the courtroom and walked to the front section to sit with the Freedom Riders when Chief Deputy Lamar Stewart knocked him to the floor and dragged

to attack segregated eateries. In early April, Albany police arrested 26 people sitting in at the Crowe Drugstore lunch counter. Twenty-four of them were teenagers and most of them were 15-16 years old. The teenagers were transported to the Camilla juvenile detention center where a number of the youngsters arrested in December had been sent.

In mid-April, Albany police violence turned deadly when an officer shot and killed Walter Harris, the African American owner and operator of the Rainbow Café. Harris was walking down the street carrying a jug of water when, according to the officer, the café owner attacked him with a knife. When the weapon was introduced into evidence at the inquest, it turned out to be an "old and rusty pocketknife." For many African Americans this story sounded too much like Gator Johnson's assault on Charlie Ware, who was still in jail in Newton awaiting trial down in Bad Baker. The following Saturday, 29 African American adults and teenagers prayed in protest outside City Hall. They were arrested and, after lying down in a gesture of passive resistance, were carried off to jail.

Direct action protest and community organizing, including the establishment of citizenship schools and voter registration—Albany had seen it all in the first half of 1962. But as Charles Sherrod looked to the future spread of the movement into rural southwest Georgia, the SNCC field secretary developed a radical plan that he shared at a regional SNCC meeting in June. The key to changing society in the rural black belt was to enfranchise African Americans. If they had the vote, they could elect political leaders who could bring about change. But direct action protest was not going to work in the heartland of white supremacy. The quick and efficient crushing of the Lee and Terrell county high school boycotts in February demonstrated to Sherrod that the

southwest Georgia—one in which black and white worked together. To strike at the root of segregation, he said, you must attack the idea of white supremacy, i.e., that white is superior to black. Interracial student teams would show that blacks and whites could work together. There was also a pragmatic reason for using interracial teams. Sherrod knew that white students would attract more media attention and consequently more federal attention to the situation in southwest Georgia.

As June ended, Sherrod and his SNCC compatriots, as well as Dr. Anderson and the Albany Movement leadership, could see some progress had been made in the previous six months. Albany businesses were hurting from the economic boycott, and there were visible cracks in the façade of white unity as moderate leaders questioned the city commission's hardline stance in negotiating with movement leaders. Citizenship schools were already adding to the number of African

As an observer noted at the time: in Lee and Terrell counties, it was "literally true that Negroes have no rights which the white man is required to respect."

strategy for bringing about change in rural southwest Georgia had to be community organizing.

To challenge the rural white power structure was an enormous task. Sherrod proposed to go into each southwest Georgia county, but he would start with the two closest and the ones he already had some experience with—Lee and Terrell. African Americans comprised 60 percent of the population in the two counties, yet no more than 50 blacks were registered to vote in either of them. As an observer noted at the time: in Lee and Terrell counties, it was "literally true that Negroes have no rights which the white man is required to respect." To work with and develop local African American leaders and to promote voter registration, Sherrod planned to send into these counties interracial teams of students. A number of people at the time may have considered such a plan insane. Yet, Sherrod had a vision for a new world in

Americans registered to vote. And the bus boycott had shut down the city bus system because Bunny Pritchett and his fellow commissioners refused to desegregate it. But Albany still remained a staunchly segregated city—schools, churches, libraries, stores, and restaurants all observed the color line. The city's elected officials refused to speak directly with African American leaders, and the media—radio, television, and the daily newspaper—was downright hostile. On June 28, for example, *Albany Herald* editor James H. Gray published a front-page editorial accusing "Albany Negro agitators" of resorting to "the Hitlerian tactic of the 'Big Lie.'" The following week, Judge Durden announced that he would hand down his decision in the Martin Luther King, Jr. trial when King showed up in his courtroom on July 10. Albanians—black and white—wondered what changes King's next visit to Albany might bring.

Martin Luther King, Jr. and Ralph Abernathy leave the Federal Courthouse in Albany, August 1962. Danny Lyon/Magnum Photos

8

For many historians, the focus of the Southwest Georgia Movement in 1962 has been on Martin Luther King's return to Albany that summer. At the same time, however, Charles Sherrod and his integrated troop of SNCC workers and volunteers opened a second front in the war on Jim Crow in the nearby plantation counties of Terrible Terrell and Lee. Needless to say, King got most of the news coverage, but the rural campaign was equally important.

King flew to Albany on July 10 for the verdict in his trial for parading without a permit in December 1961. He and Ralph Abernathy were found guilty and sentenced to 45 days in jail or a $178 fine. Although the pair chose jail, white attorney B.C. Gardner anonymously paid their fines, and they were released against their will on July 12.

nightly mass meetings, held mostly at Shiloh and Mt. Zion, King, Anderson, and other movement leaders exhorted the hundreds of attendees, but only one march took place in the 10 days following King's conviction and jailing resulting in 32 arrests. While many of these protestors languished in jail, SCLC and SNCC leaders taught daytime sessions on nonviolence tactics at Mt. Zion before sending out waves of students to desegregate the public library, parks, and pools. When 25 African American students trained by SCLC showed up at the all-white Carnegie Public Library, librarians Harold Todd and his wife turned them away. The next day 120 SNCC-trained teenagers targeted five lunch counters, Tift Park, and its pool, but were also unsuccessful.

A TWO-FRONT WAR ON JIM CROW,
Summer and Fall 1962

After his unexpected and unwanted release, King decided to stay and carry on his effort to desegregate the city. He brought in his Southern Christian Leadership Conference (SCLC) staff to coordinate the campaign. They worked in uneasy alliance with the SNCC staff led by Sherrod, Reagon, Charles Jones, and Executive Secretary James Forman, who had come down from SNCC headquarters in Atlanta. The third element ostensibly leading and holding together this restive coalition was the Albany Movement led by Dr. William Anderson and Marion Page and its energetic and dedicated secretary Goldie Jackson.

To achieve its goals of direct talks with the city commission and dismissal of the cases against the more than 800 protestors arrested since November, the Albany Movement resumed its protest marches to City Hall. It also expanded its efforts to desegregate public facilities and increased voter registration efforts. At

In the meantime, the city secured a federal court injunction against the movement and specific leaders preventing them from further protests. King, who considered the federal government an ally in the civil rights struggle, felt compelled to honor the injunction and not participate in a major march scheduled for Saturday, July 21, from Shiloh to City Hall. Others named in the injunction observed it as well. One movement leader not named in the restraining order was Rev. Samuel B. Wells, who pastored four small churches and earned a living as a sandblaster. An unpolished country preacher, Wells told some 700 crammed into Shiloh and Mt. Zion that Saturday night, "I've heard about an injunction, but I haven't seen one. I heard a few names but my name hasn't been called. But I do know where my name is being called. My name is being called on the road to freedom. I can hear the blood of Emmett Till as it calls from the ground."

Southwest Georgian *newspaper editor A.C. Searles, center, watches Albany Police Chief Laurie Pritchett address protestors before their arrest, July 11, 1962. AE Jenkins Photography*

He then called on the enthusiastic crowd to march "Now!" A few minutes after 9 p.m., 161 demonstrators, mostly teenage girls, followed Wells out of the church singing "Ain't Gonna Let Nobody Turn Me Round," a freedom song introduced in Albany earlier that month by Ralph Abernathy. Improvising, they sang, "Ain't gonna let no injunction turn me round . . ." Downtown, Police Chief Laurie Pritchett arrested all 161 protestors, many of whom were sent to jail in the outlying counties.

One of the central figures in the drama of the Albany Movement, Pritchett has gone down in history as the southern law officer who practiced nonviolence in dealing with civil rights demonstrators. He instructed his officers to handle protestors carefully without resorting to violence. Pritchett had studied Martin Luther King's Gandhian philosophy of nonviolence. King's strategy was to overwhelm the unjust system's jails by filling them with protestors, forcing the authorities to address their civil rights issues. Pritchett, however, made sure that

there was always plenty of jail space. Later in life, he spoke with pride about how he outfoxed King by renting jails from the sheriffs of the surrounding counties. There, out of the sight of the national news media, prisoners were abused and experienced the violence that Pritchett's own men in Albany avoided.

The Albany police chief could not control all the law officials in the city. On July 28, one of them, the 76-year-old sheriff of Dougherty County, D.C. "Cull" Campbell, infuriated by C.B. King's visit to check on a client, beat the African American attorney with a cane as he was leaving the sheriff's office. The bloodied lawyer (it took eight stitches to close his wound) encountered newsmen as he was leaving the courthouse, and that particular act of violence was reported in the next day's *New York Times.* Campbell admitted he had beaten King and told the FBI, "I told the son of a bitch to get out of my office, and he didn't get out." Five days earlier, Albany activist Marion (Mrs. Slater) King was visiting

Albany protestors jailed in Camilla, when she was beaten by the Mitchell County sheriff and deputy sheriff. She was pregnant at the time of the attack and later miscarried. Despite his moniker as the nonviolent police chief, Laurie Pritchett's actions and inaction contributed to violence. In the end it was not the philosophy of nonviolence that Laurie Pritchett followed, but it was the tactics of nonviolence that he so shrewdly employed.

Albany Movement attorneys appealed the federal court injunction banning demonstrations and won a temporary suspension. Once again, King got himself arrested, and after two weeks he was let go. Others joined King in jail by either protesting at City Hall or the Carnegie Library or trying to integrate a restaurant. In all, 441 protestors were arrested in Albany in July and August. In response, Chief Pritchett closed the libraries and parks "indefinitely in the interest of public safety." Among those arrested in August were two

inherent discrimination of Jim Crow, and began a two-year stint as SNCC staff photographer, launching his career as a professional lensman. Lyon's 1962 photograph of the Dougherty County Courthouse water fountains (see cover), as well as his other southwest Georgia movement pictures, are an invaluable part of the ACRI's collections.

In early August, the arch-segregationists on the city commission still adamantly refused to communicate directly with local African American leaders. When asked about Albany during a news conference on August 1, President John F. Kennedy found the situation there "wholly inexplicable." He could not understand why, if American and Soviet leaders could sit down for discussions in Geneva, white and Negro leaders could not sit down and discuss matters in Albany. Mayor Asa Kelley responded: "We agree with the president that the [city] commission . . . should discuss local problems with local nigras [sic] in an effort to reach local solutions." But the

Despite his moniker as the nonviolent police chief, Laurie Pritchett's actions and inaction contributed to violence. In the end it was not the philosophy of nonviolence that Laurie Pritchett followed, but it was the tactics of nonviolence that he so shrewdly employed.

northern white students who came south to work for SNCC—Penny Patch, an 18-year-old Swarthmore College student, and Danny Lyon, a 20-year-old University of Chicago history major. Patch worked on both the rural and urban fronts in 1962. In Albany on August 11, she tried unsuccessfully to integrate the Tift Park pool with two African American friends. Later that day, she and southern white SNCC worker Bob Zellner went to have dinner with Rev. Wells and two other African Americans at the Holiday Inn restaurant and all five were arrested for loitering.

Before he was arrested, neophyte photographer Danny Lyon got the opportunity of his career when James Forman gave him his first assignment in Albany. Forman asked Lyon, "You got a camera? Go inside the courthouse. Down at the back they have a big water cooler for whites and next to it a little bowl for Negroes. Go in there and take a picture of that." Lyon made the photograph, an iconic representation of the

city refused to talk to "outside agitators, including Martin Luther King and his coterie of troublemakers who jump about the South like so many fleas on a hot griddle and cause racial rashes where none have heretofore existed."

The two Sundays after King got out of jail on August 10, African Americans attempted to worship at several white churches. They were allowed in St. Teresa's Catholic Church, but the three trying to get in First Baptist Church (ironically the mother church of Mt. Zion) were arrested. Black worshippers were turned away without incident from six other churches. On August 20, King called on clergy around the country to come to Albany to "stand with the people of Albany as they strive for freedom." A week later, 70 religious leaders from the North and Midwest descended on Albany and were arrested for protesting. No sooner had the visiting clergy departed than 3,000 white supremacists from Georgia, Alabama, and Florida

Carolyn Daniels outside her Dawson home after it was hit by three shotgun blasts from night riders on September 5, 1962. Danny Lyon/Magnum Photos

rallied in a pasture outside Albany, reminding observers that supporters of the Ku Klux Klan here outnumbered civil rights activists.

By the end of the summer of 1962, it was clear that King had proved ineffective in desegregating Albany. Although King himself felt he had failed in Albany, African Americans in southwest Georgia knew that King's failure did not mean that the movement had failed. SNCC Field Secretary Charles Sherrod remarked that despite "how Dr. King might have felt . . . as far as we were concerned, things moved on. We didn't skip one beat."

The war against Jim Crow on the Albany front continued through the fall with efforts to desegregate the schools, enhance voter registration, and continue the economic boycott. Parents of 14 African American high school students attempted to register their children

Chatmon, but the *Albany Herald*'s drumbeat for a large white voter turnout contributed to Chatmon's loss.

The Albany Movement and SNCC workers also continued their effective boycott of white downtown and Midtown Shopping Center stores. Since a city ordinance outlawed picketing, the SNCC youth came up with the creative idea of putting messages to Boycott Downtown and Midtown on T-shirts and sweatshirts worn by high school students who "walked" rather than "demonstrated." When seven pickets supporting the boycott were arrested in December, they drove to Washington, DC and got an appointment with Department of Justice officials to discuss "the death of the First Amendment in Albany."

As important as the Albany front was in the struggle against Jim Crow in 1962, the conflict on its second front in the neighboring counties of Terrell and Lee was

Mayor Asa Kelley . . . refused to talk to "outside agitators, including Martin Luther King and his coterie of troublemakers who jump about the South like so many fleas on a hot griddle and cause racial rashes where none have heretofore existed."

at all-white Albany High School on September 4, the morning after the huge Ku Klux Klan rally. Someone hung a handwritten sign, "No Niggers, Please," at the AHS front door. School officials told the parents that pupil assignments for the new school year had already been made and could not be changed. The parents, led by Dr. Anderson, said that if the school board would not address their concerns they would sue it. Meanwhile, the Albany Movement and SNCC stepped up their voter registration efforts. Two months after King left Albany, African American businessman Thomas Chatmon secured enough votes in the election for a city commission seat to force a run-off election in November. SNCC workers and others canvassed for

Attorney C.B. King, recovering from Dougherty County Sheriff Cull Campbell's attack on July 28, 1962, consults with movement lawyers Donald Hollowell and Constance Baker Motley. AE Jenkins Photography

Arrested protestors await processing in alley (nicknamed Freedom Alley) next to the Albany city jail, Summer 1962. AE Jenkins Photography

equally significant. This second front was different in several ways from that of Albany. Not only were the outlying counties rural, the white supremacists there were more hostile, in fact murderous. Unlike the Albany front which was fought by a coalition of civil rights groups, only one group—SNCC—put troops on the ground in Terrell and Lee counties in 1962. One night that fall, SNCC organizer Charles Sherrod drove a northern white student, Jack Chatfield, on a deserted highway north of Albany. As they turned onto a dirt road, Sherrod turned to the newly arrived SNCC field secretary and stated, "This is where CORE and SCLC stop."

SNCC's Southwest Georgia Project to increase African American voter registration was what brought Sherrod and Cordell Reagon to Albany in the fall of 1961. According to Faith Holsaert, another northern white SNCC worker, Sherrod thought of the Southwest Georgia Project as "a wheel: work in the town of Albany was the hub, and organizing in the outlying counties of Lee, Terrell, and eventually Sumter, were the spokes. Together hub and spokes drove the wheel." Hence

college students who came to southwest Georgia to work with SNCC found themselves attending a mass meeting in Shiloh one night and canvassing in Terrell County the next morning. Sherrod would have preferred southern white students for his biracial teams that he sent out to talk with local farm folks. But operatives like Albany Freedom Rider and Alabama native Bob Zellner were a rarity in SNCC, so Sherrod settled for northern whites like Trinity College student Ralph Allen and Larry Rubin of Antioch College. In 1962 there were roughly a dozen SNCC workers on the Southwest Georgia Project.

When they arrived in Albany, SNCC members learned the basics of community organizing. When they went into a community to increase voter registration, they held weekly mass meetings at local churches. At these meetings they introduced the attendees to the voter registration effort, heard guest speakers, sang freedom songs, shared fellowship, and often mitigated fear. In addition, they held weekly citizenship classes where they taught people how to fill out and answer the questions on the voter registration form. SNCC workers canvassed door to door, talked to individuals one-on-one, gaining their trust and confidence; and they made return visits until they persuaded the often reluctant farm workers to come to the weekly meetings. SNCC workers were held accountable for their time and completed weekly reports on their activities that they submitted to head-quarters in Atlanta.

SNCC workers lived in the communities in which they worked, often staying in already overcrowded African American family homes. In Lee County, Penny Patch, Peggy Dammond, and Kathleen Conwell stayed with "Mama Dolly" Raines, a 65-year-old midwife, who, like Albany midwife Mary Coley, was very religious and delivered over a thousand babies—black and white. Mama Dolly was a courageous, independent woman, who sat on her front porch one particularly dangerous night "with her twelve gauge shot gun in her lap, fully loaded and a box of shells on the floor." Recalling that she had brought a number of Lee County white babies

been so happy." Working in the movement "justifies everything that happens." Watters himself, on his way to a potentially deadly confrontation between lawmen and SNCC workers at a voter registration meeting in Sasser, "never felt more alive, never more full of an energy to prevent [his death] if possible, of a comfortable confidence that, come what may, I was ready for it."

Simply canvassing for voter registration in Dawson, the Terrell County seat, could be life-threatening as Ralph Allen learned when he was physically attacked twice in July by white men upset that he was there "to show our niggers how to vote." Later that month in nearby Sasser, the Terrell and Sumter county sheriffs, several deputies and other lawmen, and a number of "disturbed white citizens" interrupted one of Sherrod's nighttime voter registration meetings in the Mount Olive Baptist Church. Besides Sherrod and Allen were Charles Jones, Penny Patch, Lucius Holloway, chair of the Terrell County voter

Years later, Larry Rubin recalled that every day in southwest Georgia [SNCC workers] were "scared shitless."

into the world, she would say with a smile, "I may have to take some of them out of this world." But the threats of violence grew so intense that even Mama Dolly finally asked Penny to leave her place and would not host any more white SNCC workers.

SNCC workers, especially in Terrell and Lee counties, lived and worked with the constant fear of violence. These counties ranked near Bad Baker in terms of the brutality faced by those—white or black—who challenged white supremacy. The fear was constant and palpable. When asked in 1962 if he was afraid, Sherrod smiled and said, "Of course. All the time." Years later, Larry Rubin recalled that every day in southwest Georgia they were "scared shitless." Even white reporters covering the movement admitted their fear of lawmen and other angry white men in rural southwest Georgia. And yet, involvement in the movement as a student activist was also powerfully satisfying. Ralph Allen, who was probably the most frequently assaulted white SNCC worker in Terrell County, told reporter Pat Watters, "I have never

registration drive, three major newspaper reporters, and 35 African Americans from Terrell, Lee, and Dougherty counties. Terrell Sheriff Zeke Mathews told the group, "We want our colored people to go on living like they have for the last hundred years." He continued, "I tell you, cap'n, we're a little fed up with this registration business." In a vivid, gripping account that appeared on the front page of the next morning's *New York Times*, reporter Claude Sitton conveyed the fear inspired by the sheriff and his accomplices: "As the 70-year-old peace officer spoke, his nephew and chief deputy, M.E. Mathews, swaggered back and forth fingering a hand-tooled black leather cartridge belt and a .38 caliber revolver. Another deputy, R.M. Dunaway, slapped a five-cell flashlight against his left palm again and again." The sheriff and his nephew harassed the group, interrogated Sherrod and Allen at length, and warned Allen to stay out of Terrell County. Meanwhile, other law officers were calling out the license plate numbers of vehicles parked outside. The air was let out of a tire and sand was put in a gas tank. True to

Rev. Samuel B. Wells leads protestors in prayer, Albany, Summer 1962. AE Jenkins Photography

form, after the terrifying interruption, Sherrod continued the meeting and concluded it with everyone singing "We Shall Overcome."

Five days after the harrowing meeting in Sasser, Sheriff Mathews arrested Sherrod and Allen in Dawson riddled their homes with bullets. Miraculously, no one was injured. The following week, Carolyn Daniels welcomed newcomer Jack Chatfield to her home in Dawson where several other SNCC workers were staying—it was Jack's first night in southwest Georgia.

Terrell Sheriff Zeke Mathews told the group, "We want our colored people to go on living like they have for the last hundred years . . . . I tell you, cap'n, we're a little fed up with this registration business."

as they accompanied African Americans registering to vote. Determined to stop voter registration efforts in neighboring Lee County, white terrorists firebombed Shady Grove Baptist Church, a SNCC voter registration meeting place, on August 15. At the end of the month, night riders went after four African Americans active in the Lee County voter registration efforts—Agnew James, Frank James, Charles Wingfield, and James Mays—and Night riders fired a series of shotgun blasts into the house, hitting Jack in the arm and grazing Prathia Hall of Temple University and Christopher Allen from England. Four days later, on September 9, two more churches were firebombed, both in Terrell County. Mount Olive was the SNCC voter registration church in Sasser that Sheriff Mathews visited in July. Mount Mary Baptist Church in Chickasawhatchee was pastored

Among those singing at the ruins of a Terrell County church burned in September 1962 are SNCC workers Prathia Hall (second from right), Ralph Allen (fourth from right) and Jack Chatfield with bandaged arm from a night rider attack on September 5. AE Jenkins Photography

by Rev. William Boyd who also pastored Union Baptist Church in Albany and was active in the movement there. A week later, a fourth church, the I Hope Baptist Church, near Dawson, was burned to the ground. "People are scared. People are crying. Some say they are going to leave Terrell," said Sherrod, but SNCC "won't be moved." He announced a voter registration meeting in Sasser in two days. The meeting would take place in a tent since the Mount Olive Church there had been destroyed.

SNCC's voter registration meeting churches were burned. Local voter registration activists' homes were shot up by night riders. And yet, with firm resolve the freedom fighters of Lee and Terrell counties persisted. At a Lee County meeting on October 31, several persons from Sumter County invited SNCC to hold a meeting at Pleasant Grove Baptist Church near De Soto. The following week SNCC held its first mass meeting in Sumter. Little did they realize that the next summer the eyes of the nation would be on the Americus Movement in Sumter's county seat.

Ruins of Mount Olive Baptist Church, Sasser, firebombed on September 9, 1962. AE Jenkins Photography

9

The Albany Movement was a people's movement that drew its support from African Americans of every class, faith, and profession. Three institutions that continue to serve as the foundation of the African American community, and which provided the resources for its massive assault on Jim Crow in the early 1960s, are the church, the family, and business. Outsiders provided the movement with some of its leadership and spiritual strength, some financial help, and some personnel critical to the movement. But the bulk of the movement's resources came from southwest Georgians—pastors and fellow church members, family members, and merchants, professionals, and other businessmen and women.

to the movement. Like most of Albany's churchgoing population, the majority of them were Baptist.

Mt. Zion Baptist Church was established in 1866 when a number of formerly enslaved members of Albany Baptist (later First Baptist) Church left the biracial church and formed the First Colored (later Mt. Zion) Baptist Church under the leadership of Rev. Ralph Watson. Mt. Zion was the site of the first Albany Movement mass meeting in November 1961. It provided space for SCLC and SNCC training sessions in summer 1962 and seats for overflow crowds from huge meetings at Shiloh across the street.

Shiloh Baptist Church was established in 1888 by several members who left Mt. Zion. It was the default

FOUNDATION OF THE ALBANY MOVEMENT: CHURCHES, FAMILIES, AND BUSINESSES

CHURCHES

The church was central to the movement in Albany and all across the South. This was where citizenship or voter registration schools and nonviolence training workshops were held as well as the all-important mass meetings. This was where testimonials were spoken by those who experienced abuse by the police and jailors. Perhaps, most important, this was where the people sang the hymns and freedom songs that gave them the courage to face the police and arrest as they marched to protest the injustices of Jim Crow. Not all churches were willing to open their doors to mass meetings. Many pastors and deacons refused because of the hostile attitudes of whites and the fear of church burnings. Two pastors early on showed courageous leadership by being the first to open their church doors to the movement's mass meetings—Rev. E. James Grant of Mt. Zion Baptist Church and Rev. H.C. Boyd of Shiloh Baptist Church. A dozen African American churches in Albany opened their doors

location for mass meetings during the movement. Most of the marches to City Hall started at Shiloh.

Mount Calvary Baptist Church was established in 1932 when Mt. Zion pastor Rev. Isaiah Harris broke away from Mt. Zion to create a new church. Harris was the father of movement activists McCree, Emory, and Rutha Harris. Mount Calvary was the site of mass meetings and was pastored by Rev. R.N. Elzia during the movement.

Bethel A.M.E. Church was established in 1867. In 1868, its pastor was Rev. Robert Crumley, an active leader in Reconstruction politics. It was the site of SNCC nonviolent workshops and training sessions. It hosted mass meetings and Dr. King met there with 70 visiting clergy in August 1962. Its pastor, Rev. Benjamin Gay, was arrested with Dr. King in July 1962.

C.K. Smith Presbyterian Church was the meeting site for the NAACP Youth Council and hosted an SCLC citizenship school. Rev. Millard F. Adams, active in the Albany branch of the NAACP, was pastor during the movement.

Restoration of all the Old Mt. Zion Baptist Church pews to their 1961 appearance was completed in 2010. Todd Stone Photography

Third Kiokee Baptist Church, one of the largest churches in Albany, was the site of mass meetings. Its pastor during the movement was Rev. R.B. Smith.

Union Baptist Church, adjacent to Albany State College, was founded in 1893 and was the site of mass meetings. Its pastor, Rev. William Boyd, was active in voter registration and other movement efforts. He also pastored Mount Mary Baptist Church, one of three Terrell County churches firebombed in September 1962.

Beulah Baptist Church, a site of mass meetings, offered sanctuary to SNCC workers whom Albany police were systematically arresting to halt protest demonstrations in summer 1963. Its pastor was Rev. J.R. Harris.

Trinity Baptist Church, the site of an SCLC citizenship class in east Albany, was pastored by Rev. L.C. Reynolds.

Greater Second Mount Olive Baptist Church, founded in 1929 and the site of mass meetings, was pastored by Rev. Jessie Johnson, father of SNCC activist and Freedom Singer Bernice Johnson.

Friendship Baptist Church, site of mass meetings and committee meetings, was pastored by Rev. J. Wesley Lowe.

Arcadia Baptist Church's pastor was Rev. Daniel Thomas. It was the site of mass meetings and provided refuge to Randy Battle and two other black men who scaled the fence and jumped into the all-white Tift Park pool in July 1963.

FAMILIES

When students and ministers and others came from all over the U.S. to assist with voter registration and to march in protest, many local families took them in, fed them, and gave them a place to sleep. Since there were far too many families to include here, a few examples of those who were also very active in the movement will have to suffice:

The C.W. King Family

Clennon W. and Margaret Slater King were graduates of Tuskegee Institute where C.W. had earned expenses working as a "buggy boy" for Tuskegee President Booker T. Washington. The Kings had seven sons, all of them highly educated. The family was very active in civil rights. C.W. was involved in establishing the Albany branch of the NAACP and the local Voters League. Two of the sons—Slater, a real estate broker, and C.B., one of three black attorneys in Georgia outside Atlanta—were heavily involved in the Albany Movement. Vice president of the movement, Slater was arrested in a December 1961 demonstration and beaten in the Albany jail. His wife Marion, who was pregnant, was assaulted in Camilla by the Mitchell County sheriff in July 1962. Her brother-in-law, C.B. King, who litigated numerous civil rights cases in southwest Georgia, was beaten in Albany in July 1962 by the Dougherty County sheriff. The new federal courthouse in downtown Albany was named in his honor in 2002.

The James Christian Family

James and Odessa Mae Christian and their four young daughters were heavily involved in the Albany Movement. The first to get arrested was their 14-year-old daughter Joann, who, by age 16, had been jailed 17 times. In summer 1963, she was arrested and brutally beaten before being sent to Camilla where she was kept in solitary confinement. Her sister Lavetta and a cousin were also arrested and put in solitary. Lavetta was molested and the girls heard threats like "We're gonna kill all them Christian bitches." When she got out of jail, she found her father and her cousin Monroe Gaines armed and guarding SNCC workers who had sought sanctuary inside Shiloh. Later that year, Joann and her 9-year-old sister James Zemma Christian testified in the trial of the Albany Nine. In 1964 Joann was one of the first six African Americans to integrate Albany High School. Joann believes her family's involvement in the movement was a family calling. The many SNCC workers and other civil rights volunteers who were housed and fed by the Christian family would agree.

The Isaiah A. Harris Family

Rev. Isaiah A. and Katie B. Harris came to Albany in 1929 when Rev. Harris became pastor of Mt. Zion Baptist Church. He left Mt. Zion in 1932 and founded Mount Calvary Baptist Church. Before his death in 1951, he had encouraged African Americans to register to vote and set up a literacy school at Mount Calvary to better prepare people for registration. The children—Emory, Alphonso, Elijah, McCree, Rosetta, Juanita, and Rutha—were all involved in the movement. The Harris residence was a freedom house that provided lodging, food, encouragement, and support to numerous out-of-town volunteers and SNCC workers. McCree used her position as Latin and French teacher at Monroe High School to quietly alert student activists when they were needed at Shiloh for an impending march or demonstration. Rutha and Emory used the gift of their voices to sing for civil rights. Rutha was one of the original four SNCC Freedom Singers who traveled the country giving concerts to raise money for SNCC.

Two pastors early on showed courageous leadership by being the first to open their church doors to the movement's mass meetings— Rev. E. James Grant of Mt. Zion Baptist Church and Rev. H.C. Boyd of Shiloh Baptist Church.

The Monroe Gaines Family

Monroe and Lorenzo Gaines and their four daughters marched and spent time in jail. They housed many of the SNCC workers, including Penny Patch. Three of the children and their father were named as plaintiffs in the lawsuit brought against the Dougherty County Board of Education. By age 15, Patricia Gaines had been arrested and jailed more than a dozen times. In August 1964, one month after President Lyndon Johnson signed into law the Civil Rights Act of 1964, she and her friend Margaret Sanders went to the Dougherty County Courthouse and stole the "White" and "Colored" signs at the water fountains. They later gave the "Colored" sign as a gift to Penny Patch, who eventually moved to Vermont. When she heard about the new civil rights museum that was going to open in the Old Mt. Zion Church in 1998, Penny donated the sign and it has been a treasured part of our collection ever since.

The Leonard Lawrence Family

Leonard and Eunice Lawrence lost their jobs because of their participation in the Albany Movement. Their children were also named in the lawsuit against the Dougherty County Board of Education. Shirley Lawrence was one of the first six African Americans to integrate Albany High School in 1964 and endured a year of harassment from white students and teachers.

BUSINESSES

Many African American and a few white businesses supported the Albany Movement. African American businesses provided their proprietors a certain amount of independence since they did not depend on white customers for their income. Businessmen contributed money, in-kind support, professional expertise, and personal support to the movement. A number of them housed out-of-town supporters and posted bond for jailed protestors who could not afford their bail.

Colored Sign removed from the Dougherty County Courthouse by Patricia Gaines and Margaret Sanders in August 1964 and given to SNCC worker Penny Patch who donated it to the Albany Civil Rights Movement Museum in 1998. It is now adjacent to the "Churches, Families and Businesses" exhibit at ACRI. Todd Stone Photography

Harlem Barber Shop was co-owned by four men, including barber Robert Thomas, one of the Albany Nine indicted in 1963.

Cochran Studio was owned by Benjamin F. Cochran (1912-1996), the official photographer of the movement, who documented numerous movement activities with his camera.

Dr. J. H. Ellis, Dentist, was an Albany native and a graduate of Meharry Medical College. He had a lucrative practice and contributed financially to the movement. He also put up out-of-town supporters, including SNCC activists Diane Nash and her husband James Bevel.

George and Son Grocery and Market was established in the late 1940s by O.C. George (1914-1952) and his wife

Slater [King] was arrested . . . and beaten in the Albany jail. His wife Marion, who was pregnant, was assaulted in Camilla by the Mitchell County sheriff in July 1962. Her brother-in-law, C.B. King . . . was beaten in Albany in July 1962 by the Dougherty County sheriff.

Chatmon's Beauty and Barber Supplies was owned by Thomas Chatmon, adult supervisor of the local NAACP Youth Council. He ran for a seat on the Albany city commission in fall 1962 and won enough votes to trigger a runoff election. In 1963 he was indicted as one of the Albany Nine.

The George H. Elliott Mortuary, the first African American funeral home in Albany, was established in 1900. Owners George and Corine Elliott loaned Dr. Anderson a new Cadillac to drive Dr. King to Atlanta and back to Albany.

Irene. O.C. was an active NAACP member and a vigorous advocate of voter registration. Irene George, who ran the grocery at the time of the movement, posted bond for arrested protestors and opened her home to out-of-town supporters.

Price's Barber Shop was owned by Thornton Price, who attended mass meetings, helped fundraise for the movement, and drove a station wagon full of people from Albany to the 1963 March on Washington.

Poteat Funeral Home, owned by Walter Poteat and located on the same block of Whitney Avenue as Shiloh and

Mt. Zion churches, served as a media center for news reporters calling in their stories after mass meetings. The Poteat ambulance service carried arrested protestors needing hospitalization from the Lee County Stockade to Phoebe Putney Memorial Hospital in Albany.

Dr. J.P. Cheevers, Dentist, lived on the same block of Whitney Avenue as Shiloh and Mt. Zion churches next door to wealthy planter Bartow Powell whom he knew growing up. Dr. Cheevers (1906-1991) began his practice in Albany around 1935, was treasurer of Bethel A.M.E. Church for 45 years, and was an active member of the NAACP Albany branch.

Rabbitman's, a shoeshine shop, was operated by Elijah "Rabbitman" Williams in the early 1960s. Rabbitman marched and was jailed a half-dozen times.

Odom's Gulf Services, the first African American service station franchise in Albany, donated gasoline to carpool drivers during the bus boycott.

As a result of the unified front of the white community

first African American employee to a permanent supervisory position. Several years later, company executive Bee McCormack learned that very few of the company's black employees were registered to vote due largely to their fear of the literacy test. So McCormack and another white employee coached a small group of African American workers and McCormack accompanied them to the courthouse where they all passed the test and registered. Soon, other black employees were similarly prepared and successfully registered. Bobs Candies's quiet support of voter registration as well as its financial contributions to the movement led many to consider it an ally and supporter of the movement.

The Albany Movement's attack on Jim Crow, however, impacted Bobs's African American employees and revealed just how southern and white this progressive company was. In December 1961, as hundreds of black Albanians were getting arrested and jailed, the president of Bobs cancelled the traditional segregated Christmas parties. The following fall, after a brief walkout by African American employees,

Lee King . . . discovered one of the more bizarre aspects of Jim Crow: the company ordered different toilet paper for blacks and whites. "White restrooms had soft paper and the blacks' had rough dark paper. You could see the bark in it."

against integration, there were few white businesses in Albany sympathetic to the movement. Two of them operated in Harlem, the African American business district. **Giles Grocery** was the only white-owned grocery store that hired black cashiers. **Jimmies Hot Dogs** supported the movement by providing no preferential treatment to white customers. **Seeley's Printing Company** also hired several black employees and printed flyers for the movement. But the company had to do this surreptitiously after hours.

Bobs Candies is a good example of the challenges a progressive white-owned southern company faced in dealing with race during the civil rights era. Bobs Candies began in downtown Albany in 1919 and steadily grew so that by the 1990s it was the largest manufacturer of candy canes in the world. Between 1953 and 1956 the number of employees increased from 225 to 310. As the only company in Albany that hired blacks for production line jobs, it had access to some of the best workers in the African American labor force in Dougherty County. In 1954, Bobs appointed its

Bobs secured a new personnel director Lee King. King interviewed a number of black workers and learned of their unhappiness with segregated dressing rooms, restrooms, and water fountains. They told him how whites were served first in the cafeteria getting "the choice pieces of fried chicken." Then he discovered one of the more bizarre aspects of Jim Crow: the company ordered different toilet paper for blacks and whites. "White restrooms had soft paper and the blacks' had rough dark paper. You could see the bark in it." To its credit, Bobs moved quickly to address these complaints. By the end of 1962, it had desegregated its restrooms (with one kind of toilet paper), dressing rooms, and water fountains, and had established a biracial committee to discuss problems.

Local churches, families, and businesses in Albany and the surrounding counties were the foundation on which the movement stood, and they were essential to its success. The life and spirit of the movement, however, came from its music which shaped in a very special way the southwest Georgia protests.

Freedom Songs were an integral part of mass meetings held in churches like Third Kiokee Baptist Church in Albany, Summer 1962.
Danny Lyon/Magnum Photos

10

Music and song played a powerful role in the southwest Georgia freedom struggle. At the time, SNCC leader Charles Jones remarked, "There could have been no Albany Movement without music." According to Police Chief Laurie Pritchett, even the jail guards who were booking the hundreds of protestors in December 1961 were singing and humming along with the arrested marchers. An unsympathetic white onlooker who heard their "Freedom Chant" described it as "hair-raising." Reporter Pat Watters said the music he experienced the summer of 1962 in Shiloh and Mt. Zion Baptist churches could not "be described—or recaptured. It was there. I heard it, was privileged to hear it night after night in the packed-in heat" with his dripping sweat smudging his hastily scribbled notes. A half-century

congregational leaders offered up prayers between songs. Pastors and other preachers prayed and sermonized and their song-sermons were a vital part of mass meetings. On occasion, someone recently released from jail would give testimony of her prison experiences. Albany Movement leaders kept a steady flow of cash into their coffers by making sure the plate was passed at each mass meeting. The talking was important, but it was the singing that had the greatest impact on those attending.

The freedom songs for which the Albany Movement became famous derived from several sources: the African American church, the labor movement and popular culture. Most of the songs, particularly the ones sung at mass meetings, came directly from traditional African American religious music—gospel, spirituals, and hymns.

MUSIC AND THE MOVEMENT

later, SNCC worker Peter de Lissovoy recalled, "There is something almost indescribable to me about the music and singing, its sources and effects, and I can hardly get my mind around the part music and singing played on a daily basis in everything! It was a powerful mysterious inner current of motivation and encouragement and solace and confidence. The music was almost like the ground beneath our feet."

Freedom songs were sung at SNCC meetings, on protest marches, in jail, and while canvassing, but the most prominent place people experienced the power of the music was at the mass meetings. SNCC worker Prathia Hall could hear the voices singing and the feet rhythmically stomping for some distance as she approached the mass meetings in Albany. Mass meetings consisted of singing, praying, preaching, testifying, and passing the collection plate, but more singing was done than anything else. Deacons, church mothers, and other

One of the earliest song leaders in the Albany Movement, Bernice Johnson Reagon, went on to become a leading scholarly authority on traditional African American music. Much of the movement music reflected the congregational style of singing found in many rural black Baptist churches in southwest Georgia. The music was unrehearsed; it was not performed solo or by a choral group. Instead, a song leader started a song and the congregation joined in. In a sense, the music came out of the congregation from the seed planted by the song leader. And in southwest Georgia, particularly, the singing was a capella.

The role of the song leader in congregational singing was critical. The leader began the song and, with the right blend of energy and enthusiasm, inspired the congregation to fall in and make the song happen. Song leaders often led by "raising a song" or "lining," i.e., calling out the first line of a song and then the congregation joined in with the rest of the lyrics. Many of the freedom songs were

The original SNCC Freedom Singers founded in Albany, December 1962. Left to right: Charles "Chuck" Neblett, Rutha Mae Harris, Bernice Johnson, and Cordell Reagon. Bobby Burch Collection.

church songs with some or all of the words changed to relate to freedom and to the local community in which they were sung.

The first freedom songs of the modern civil rights movement came out of the 1960 student sit-ins in the Carolinas and Nashville. The Freedom Riders in 1961 added to this repertoire. When SNCC organizers came to a new community, they taught local people freedom songs. One of the first things Sherrod and Cordell Reagon did when they came to Albany in October 1961 was to teach freedom songs to high school and college students in the NAACP Youth Council. Sherrod, Reagon and Charles Jones were among the song leaders when the mass meetings began after Thanksgiving. ASC student Bernice Johnson and Florida A & M University student Rutha Harris quickly emerged as the most outstanding song leaders. Others included ASC students Bertha Gober, Janie Culbreth, Andrew Reid, Larry Gibson, Brenda Darden, and Annette Jones, all of whom were suspended or expelled from ASC in December for civil rights activities. In 1963, nine-year-old James Zemma Christian and her seven-year-old sister Deloris were the song leaders at a mass meeting. In Sumter County that year, Amanda Bowens,

Virginia Davis, and Sammy Mahone emerged as Americus song leaders.

The history of each freedom song, how it came to Albany or how it started there, and how it was modified in southwest Georgia is fascinating. Rev. Osby of Aurora, Illinois, was in jail in Jackson, Mississippi, during the Freedom Rides in 1961 when he revised the lyrics of a gospel quartet song, "I Woke Up This Morning with My Mind Stayed on Jesus," creating the vibrant and energizing "I Woke Up This Morning with My Mind Stayed on Freedom." Sherrod and Reagon brought it from Mississippi to Albany in fall 1961. They also brought "Keep Your Eyes on the Prize," a song whose obscure origins as an African American song, "Gospel Plow," stretch back to the early twentieth century. One version of the song is known as "Keep Your Hand on the Plow." In the 1950s, Guy Carawan of the Highlander Folk School encountered a newer version, "Keep Your Eyes on the Prize," in one of Septima Clark's citizenship schools on Johns Island, SC. The song resonated with the students in the 1960 sit-ins and with the Freedom Riders in 1961. "Keep Your Eyes on the Prize" caught on quickly in Albany, and at the first mass arrest in December 1961, marchers sang it as they went to jail.

Two weeks earlier, on Monday, November 27, the first freedom song created in Albany was born. That day, Bernice Johnson and Annette Jones led their fellow ASC students on a large march protesting the trial of the five students who had tried to desegregate the Trailways Bus Station the day before Thanksgiving. Instead of returning directly to campus, the students met at Union Baptist Church, adjacent to ASC. There, SNCC leader Charles Jones turned to Bernice Johnson and said, "Bernice, sing a song." She "took a breath and started 'Over My Head, I See Trouble in the Air.' As I moved down that first line, I knew it would not be a good idea to sing the word trouble, even though I knew we were in trouble, but did not think it would help. So instead I put in freedom, and by the second line everyone was singing, with me placing a new word (glory, justice, and so forth) for each cycle:

> Over my head, I see freedom in the air
> Over my head, I see freedom in the air
> Over my head, I see freedom in the air
> There must be a God somewhere.

Chief Laurie Pritchett to release the hundreds incarcerated that week. In place of the traditional lyrics,

> Oh Mary, Oh Martha,
> Oh Mary, come ring them bells

Janie wrote,

> Oh Pritchett, Oh Kelley
> Oh Pritchett, open them cells.

Since Bertha was the better singer, she took the lead as the two of them sang out their plea in call and response style. Others joined in with other spirituals and eventually they were released when Dr. King and city officials came to their verbal agreement. And "Oh Pritchett, Oh Kelley" entered the canon of Albany freedom songs.

The following June, SNCC workers John Lewis, Carver "Chico" Neblett, and Freedom Rider Salynn McCollum were organizing in Cairo, Illinois, when Chico rewrote the words to another traditional song, "Oh Mary

According to Police Chief Laurie Pritchett, even the jail guards who were booking the hundreds of protestors in December 1961 were singing and humming along with the arrested marchers.

"It was the first time I'd ever changed the text of a sacred song," said Bernice. "It was the beginning of my understanding how to use what I'd been given in that body of old songs we had learned growing up in school and church. . . . At that moment in Union Baptist I claimed these sacred songs truly as my own. . . . I could change the text to articulate and support what we were trying to do in fighting segregation."

Two of Bernice Johnson's fellow ASC students, in jail the week of the mass arrests in December, followed Bernice's example of making a sacred song their own. Bertha Gober had been arrested along with the Freedom Riders at the train station on Sunday, December 10, and Janie Culbreth was one of the 267 arrested in the first mass march on Tuesday, December 12. Both of them ended up in the overcrowded city jail. After languishing there for three days, Janie turned the spiritual "Rockin' Jerusalem" into a plea to Mayor Asa Kelley and Police

Don't You Weep," turning it into the freedom song, "If You Miss Me at the Back of the Bus":

> If you miss me at the back of the bus, and
>   you can't find me nowhere
> Come on over to the front of the bus,
>   I'll be riding up there.

Within weeks, the new freedom song had made it to Albany, and SNCC leader Charles Jones incorporated it into his training workshop for teenage demonstrators at Mt. Zion on July 18. Before sending them out to integrate Tift Park, he led them in singing:

> If you miss me at Carver Park, and you can't
>   find me nowhere
> Just come on over to Tift Park pool, I'll be
>   swimming over there

Similarly, Rev. Ralph David Abernathy asked those attending a mass meeting to meet at 2 o'clock at Mt. Zion and Shiloh. Mirthfully, he stated, "Now if you meet me down at Mt Zion," and then breaking into song:

And you can't find me nowhere
Then you come on down to city jail, because
    I'll be waitin' down there.
If you meet me down at city jail, and you can't
    find me nowhere
Then you come on up to Camilla, because they
    will have transferred me over there

Abernathy, himself, introduced a traditional song at a mass meeting at Mt. Zion in July 1962 that quickly became the anthem of the southwest Georgia movement:

Ain't gonna let nobody turn me 'round, turn me
    'round, turn me 'round,
Ain't gonna let nobody turn me 'round,
I'm gonna keep on a walkin', keep on a talkin',
    marching up to freedom land

jail for his part in the Freedom Rides, Congress of Racial Equality (CORE) Executive Director James Farmer rewrote Reece's lyrics. Sherrod and Reagon brought Farmer's new freedom song with them to Albany and soon it had new verses:

They say in Dougherty County, no neutrals
    have we met
You'll either be a freedom fighter or a Tom for
    Chief Pritchett
My Lordy, which side are you on, boy? Which
    side are you on?

Oh tell me Mayor Kelley, where is your heart?
We are all children of the Almighty God
My Lordy, which side are you on, boy? Which
    side are you on?

Other spirituals or church songs that came to the civil rights movement via the 1930s and 1940s labor organizing efforts include "Oh Freedom," "We Shall Not Be Moved," and the theme song of the movement, "We

One of the first things Sherrod and Cordell Reagon did when they came to Albany in October 1961 was to teach freedom songs to high school and college students in the NAACP Youth Council.

Subsequent verses began "Ain't gonna let Chief Pritchett turn me 'round," "Ain't gonna let Mayor Kelley . . .," "Ain't gonna let segregation . . .," and so on. When the song was sung in Terrell County, a verse was added for Sheriff Z.T. Mathews: "Ain't gonna let Z.T. turn me 'round."

Although religious songs were the source of many freedom songs, some of them did not come directly from church but took a circuitous route through the labor movement. One of the most famous of the labor songs, "Which Side Are You On?" was written during the Harlan County, Kentucky, coal miners' strike in 1931 by Florence Reece, the wife of a union organizer. For the melody, Reece turned to a traditional Baptist hymn, "Lay the Lily Low." Thirty years later, while in

Shall Overcome." Reagon and Sherrod taught the youth in Albany the ritual of standing while singing "We Shall Overcome," holding hands with your right arm crossed over your left. Mass meetings usually closed with this song. Marchers walking to City Hall sang it. African Americans, intimidated by the Terrell and Sumter county sheriffs and their deputies at a Sasser church meeting in July 1962, began humming "We Shall Overcome" to give themselves the strength and courage to endure the harassment.

If music helped give protestors the courage they needed to go to jail, it was also what sustained them in jail. Prisoners often sang a good part of the night. A white SNCC worker arrested with a number of black protestors in June 1963 recalled, "The first night we on the white side of Albany jail and about 30 on the black side sang most of the night and the music integrated the jail, really. It was something." Jailors and sheriffs recognized the power of the freedom songs and, in the Dawson and Camilla jails, singing was forbidden. It was a different story in Albany where Chief Pritchett asked jailed freedom singer Rutha Harris to sing that song about Mayor Kelley and him.

Everyone connected to the movement recognized what a gift its music was—how it empowered people of color and their handful of white allies in southwest Georgia to challenge the oppression of Jim Crow in Albany and the surrounding counties. It soon became clear to movement leaders that this gift could be shared with a wider audience outside the region that could provide support to the southwest Georgia movement. Once again it was SNCC who took the lead in this effort.

Working with Guy Carawan and Alan Lomax, SNCC produced an LP record album entitled *Freedom in the Air, a documentary on Albany, Georgia, 1961-1962.* Manufactured in fall 1962, the album contained

rich African American musical tradition of the Albany area led him to support the newly formed SNCC Freedom Singers organized by Cordell Reagon. The group consisted of Reagon, Bernice Johnson, Rutha Harris, and Charles "Chuck" Neblett. Singing with the group occasionally were Chuck's brother Chico (who had written "If You Miss Me at the Back of the Bus") and Bertha Gober. Seeger introduced the ensemble at a concert in Atlanta in November. Afterwards, he spent four hours with them recording a number of their songs.

The SNCC Freedom Singers toured the country—50,000 miles, 46 states—in nine months, performing over 100 concerts raising money for SNCC. SNCC worker Bobby Burch, one of the suspended ASC students, drove the troupe in a compact Buick donated by folksinger Len Dresslar. One of the high points of their nationwide tour was their June 1963 performance at Carnegie Hall where they shared the stage with the incomparable Mahalia Jackson before an audience of over 2,000. *New York Times* music critic Robert Shelton called the SNCC Freedom Singers "the ablest perform-

The SNCC Freedom Singers toured the country—50,000 miles, 46 states—in nine months, performing over 100 concerts raising money for SNCC.

recordings of traditional hymns, freedom songs as well as narration by Marion Page and Charles Sherrod and a rousing sermon by Rev. Ben Gay. The album was a fundraiser for SNCC and received a stellar review by the *New York Times* which called it "the most effective documentary recording to grow out of the integration movement."

Around the same time, New Yorkers had the opportunity to hear the leading Albany freedom song artist perform at Carnegie Hall. On September 22, folk musician Pete Seeger presided over *Sing Out* magazine's annual Hootenanny. Among the 20 folk musicians performing was Bernice Johnson who "stole the show" with her freedom songs and traditional African American music. Seeger's interest in promoting SNCC and the

ing group to come out of what is perhaps the most spontaneous and widespread singing movement in the world today. Their message was delivered in a stirring fashion, musically and morally."

A second SNCC Freedom Singers group was formed in 1964 and included Cordell Reagon and Chuck Neblett from the original group. When the Albany Civil Rights Movement Museum opened in 1998, original Freedom Singer Rutha Harris formed a new adult choir to perform freedom songs for museum visitors. Today the ACRI Freedom Singers perform the second Saturday each month so that visitors can experience for themselves the power of southwest Georgia freedom music.

Charles Sherrod, center, in Dawson, Georgia, 1963. Danny Lyon/Magnum Photos

11

For many historians, the Albany Movement was a 1961-1962 affair, commencing with Martin Luther King, Jr.'s arrival in southwest Georgia and concluding with his departure. We have already seen how the roots of 1961-1962 reach back more than a century. A closer look at the post-1962 era suggests a continuation of the freedom struggle that has been largely ignored in historical accounts.

In 1963-1966 the civil rights movement continued in Albany and Terrell and Lee counties and expanded to much of the rest of southwest Georgia, especially towns like Americus, Moultrie, Bainbridge, Newton, and Cordele. Hundreds were involved in public protest marches, sit-ins, and voter registration efforts; many were arrested and jailed. Albany was the hotspot in early summer 1963 when close to 300 were arrested. Later in the summer the focus shifted

victory for the movement. But the reality was that the city retained segregation through ordinances prohibiting disorderly conduct and loitering. The city reopened the white Carnegie Public Library on an integrated basis, but with the chairs removed so that whites would not have to endure African American patrons sitting next to them. In June, to avoid integrating the Tift Park pool and tennis court, the city sold them to the arch-segregationist editor of the *Albany Herald*, James Gray. According to Peter de Lissovoy, who had dropped out of Harvard and come to Albany to work with SNCC, "For the Movement kids in summer 1963 . . . the main issue and the hot topic was that segregated swimming pool in Tift Park."

De Lissovoy joined his Harvard classmate John Perdew and a number of northern white students, recruited by

GAINS AND LOSSES IN ALBANY, AMERICUS, AND SURROUNDING COUNTIES,
1963-1966

to Americus where over 250 were jailed. Meanwhile, the federal government went on the offensive and attacked the Albany Movement by indicting the Albany Nine.

1963 started out with the release on bond of Charlie Ware who had been wasting away in the Baker County jail for assaulting Sheriff Gator Johnson. The sheriff shot the handcuffed Ware in his cruiser in July 1961, but it was Ware who was jailed. The courageous field hand, with the help of African American attorney C.B. King, sued Gator Johnson in federal court in April for violating his civil rights. Representing the sheriff was Mayor Asa Kelley's law partner B.C. Gardner. An all-white jury in Albany found in favor of the sheriff. The future did not look promising for Charlie Ware as he looked ahead to the summer and his own trial in Baker County for assaulting the sheriff.

The month before the *Ware v. Johnson* case was tried, the Albany city commission removed all the segregation statutes from its books which at first appeared to be a

Charles Sherrod to work on SNCC's Southwest Georgia Project, at an orientation session at Koinonia on June 16. Within days they were marching in their first antisegregation protest to the newly privatized Tift Park pool. They never made it to the pool that evening. Police cars and a paddy wagon appeared and, before they knew it 26 were arrested, including Perdew and de Lissovoy. The two neophytes were among six who were initially taken to the city jail and then transferred to the Lee County jail where they went on a hunger strike for 21 days. Another new white recruit to visit the Albany city jail that week was law student Dennis Roberts, an intern for C.B. King. "The cells," he reported, "are unbelievably filthy; smells of human excrement overwhelm you on entering. Puddles of water covered the floor and the Negro girls complained of having water sprayed on them by the police."

The nighttime arrests began three days of demonstrations in which over 140 were arrested, including 20 of the 25

The "Lost Girls," teenagers arrested in Americus protests, Summer 1963, and jailed in the Lee County Stockade. Standing facing camera left to right: Linda Brown, Janet Broner, Mattie Criton, Pearl Brown, Carol Broner, Ann Ragins, Willie Mae Smith, Zelda Whitehead (or Lulu Westbrooks), Billie Jo Thornton. Seated on floor at right: Vernon Hollis. Rear, center, facing left in front of window: Goldie Mae Harris. Identifications by Billie Thornton Allen. Danny Lyon/Magnum Photos

SNCC field secretaries in southwest Georgia. The remaining SNCC workers moved into Shiloh where they slept on pews to avoid arrest. On July 6, the Ku Klux Klan held a rally southeast of town where Albany Municipal Judge Clayton Jones warned the 300 gathered, 50 of them "in sheets," of the "Communist-inspired" desegregation movement. Arguing that the "Negroes' objective was intermarriage," the local judge, who regularly sentenced civil rights protestors to jail, urged his listeners to "hurl back that black tide that's trying to engulf you and take over this country." Georgia Klan leader Calvin F. Craig then advised the crowd on how to handle African Americans boycotting Albany merchants: "If these niggers here in Dougherty County lays down in front of a store, don't walk around them. . . . Step on 'em and go in there and trade with that man!"

The day after the Klan rally, the Tift Park pool reopened as a private facility for whites only. Several protestors were arrested, including Slater King, who had succeeded Dr. Anderson as Albany Movement president. The next day,

Rev. Samuel B. Wells and 11 others marched to City Hall to protest the pool's whites only policy. They were arrested and Wells was dragged by his genitals into the police station. The following Saturday, Randy Battle, Jake Wallace, and gang leader James Daniel executed what in SNCC lore became known as the "Great Pool Jump." Randy and James had become SNCC supporters and, that day, while six protestors were being arrested for trying to buy pool tickets, the three young men scaled the pool fence and plunged fully clothed into the water, swam across the pool, climbed out, exited the back gate, and ran to nearby Arcadia Church.

Randy later recalled that when they hit the water, "them white folks and kids went straight up in the air, they didn't climb out, they . . . *flew* over to the sides. . . . I bet you in half a minute there wasn't nobody in the pool but the three of us. And they started screaming and hollering, 'Niggas! Niggas!'" Randy noted that "they drained that pool and spent three days . . . . down there scrubbing with hand brushes . . . every inch."

The same day as the Great Pool Jump and 40 miles to the north in Sumter County, 17 persons were arrested trying to buy tickets at the Martin Theater's white entrance in Americus. SNCC had been engaged in voter registration efforts in Sumter for six months. SNCC workers Don Harris and Ralph Allen had developed a real following among the Americus students whose marching and picketing increased as the summer wore on—in July over 50 had been arrested and jailed. John Perdew, fresh off his 21-day hunger strike in Lee County jail, joined Harris and Allen to work with the expanding movement in Americus. The three SNCC workers were arrested outside the Friendship Baptist Church after a mass meeting on August 8 and charged with inciting insurrection, a capital offense. Americus authorities used the state's 1871 anti-insurrection law since persons charged with a capital offense could not be bailed out of jail. Americus whites thus decapitated the SNCC leadership in Sumter County, at least until their trial. The following week CORE activist Zev Aelony was

confinement. He developed the pictures and sent them to a member of Congress and the resulting publicity led to the girls' release.

While Albany and Americus jails swallowed up large numbers of teenage protestors in July, Charlie Ware faced his Baker County trial for assaulting Gator Johnson. C.B. King and Donald Hollowell, the two most prominent African American attorneys in the state, comprised the defense's legal team. The state solicitor was assisted by Albany attorney B.C. Gardner, who had represented the Baker County sheriff when Ware sued him three months earlier. This time the trial was in Newton at the Baker County Courthouse, outside of which the sheriff had shot the handcuffed Ware in the officer's cruiser. Despite the best efforts of King and Hollowell, there was no way an all-white Baker County jury would find for a black man accused of assaulting the sheriff. At the conclusion of the four-day trial, the jury found Ware guilty but recommended that the charges be reduced to a misdemeanor. The judge rejected the

Randy [Battle] later recalled that when they hit the water, "them white folks and kids went straight up in the air, they didn't climb out, they . . . *flew* over to the sides. . . . I bet you in half a minute there wasn't nobody in the pool but the three of us."

arrested and also charged with inciting insurrection. Soon the Americus Four became an international cause célèbre. The four civil rights workers took Americus officials to federal court where on November 1 a three-judge panel ruled the insurrection statute unconstitutional and ordered the release of the four activists.

Within days of the arrest of the three SNCC workers in August, over 200 mostly young protestors were arrested in Americus. Many of the teenage girls, some as young as 13, were processed and then sent to Lee County, eventually ending up at the old Lee County Stockade. The girls' parents were not notified of their location and the Americus police were no help in locating the "lost girls." The stockade was a disgusting run-down building with one toilet clogged with feces and one source of water, a dripping shower head. The girls were fed hamburgers once a day. SNCC photographer Danny Lyon, came down from Atlanta, snuck around the back of the stockade, and took photographs of the girls and the horrific conditions of their

jury's recommendation and it looked like Ware would return to the Baker County jail while his case was appealed. Fearing for Ware's life back in Gator's bailiwick, one of Baker County's more prosperous African American farmers, Hosie Miller, signed a property bond which allowed Ware to return to his home in Albany.

In the meantime, it was events connected to Ware's April trial, in which he sued Gator Johnson and lost, that became the basis for an attack by the federal government on the leadership of the Albany Movement in the case of the Albany Nine. On the jury, which ruled in the sheriff's favor, was Carl Smith. Smith was the white proprietor of a grocery store in Harlem, Albany's black business district. The Albany Movement had been picketing Smith's and two other white-owned grocery stores in Harlem for not hiring African Americans as clerks and cashiers. First local, and then federal, authorities viewed the picketing of Smith's store as the Albany Movement trying to punish Smith for his jury vote in the Ware case. This turned into

RUBYE NELL SINGLETON

MAMIE

JOANN CHRISTIAN

BEVERLY

TRAILBLAZERS IN THE
EQUAL EDUCATIONAL O
Albany High School, C

Six African American young women, the first students to integrate Albany High School,1964-1965, were sketched years later by a white classmate Nancy Jones Presley, based on their yearbook photographs. Framed and donated to ACRI by the artist.

accusations of obstruction of justice that ultimately led to federal indictments of the Albany Nine in August. Indicted for perjury during the federal grand jury investigation of the case were: Albany Movement President Slater King, Albany Movement Secretary Elza "Goldie" Jackson, Rev. Samuel B. Wells, businessman Thomas Chatmon, barber Robert Thomas, and white SNCC worker Joni Rabinowitz. Indicted for obstruction of justice were Albany Movement founding President William G. Anderson, 16-year-old high school activist Luther Woodall, and Robert "New York" Colbert.

As with the Americus Four, the Albany Nine became a cause célèbre. For many, the motive appeared the same—attack the movement by jailing its leadership. It was bad enough when local whites engaged in this behavior. Until the Albany Nine indictments, the federal government was perceived by some in the movement as an ally or at least

Placing third was architect Edward Vason Jones, who described himself as a "Goldwater conservative." The fact that the moderate white and African American outpolled the white hardliner hinted at a softening of arch-segregationist control of Albany politics.

Six months after Slater King lost the mayoral race in Albany, his brother C.B. King qualified for the Democratic nomination for the second congressional district which covered 22 southwest Georgia counties. Campaigning in this region could be a real challenge. The previous summer, Dennis Roberts, the C.B. King intern, tore down at great risk several campaign signs of Terrell County Judge "W.I. (Don't Want the Nigger Vote) Geer." King's advance team consisted of Randy Battle and Rev. McKendrick (with Peter de Lissovoy substituting for the preacher on occasion). Their job was to go to the various towns and hamlets where C.B. would campaign and line up the venue,

As with the Americus Four, the Albany Nine became a cause célèbre. For many, the motive appeared the same—attack the movement by jailing its leadership.

neutral. But now it appeared, as one older black Albanian lamented, that "even the federal government is a white man." The six indicted for perjury were tried and convicted, but the cases were appealed and eventually overturned in 1966. Dr. Anderson, who had moved to Detroit, returned to Albany for trial which ended in a hung jury. His case was transferred to Detroit where he pled nolo contendere and was placed on unsupervised probation for one year. His felony conviction was later expunged from his record.

A key element of the freedom struggle in the 1960s was the voter registration campaigns in Dougherty, Lee, Terrell, and Sumter counties and eventually all of southwest Georgia. One way to increase voter registration was to offer African American voters black candidates to elect. Voter registration increased in Albany in fall 1962 when Thomas Chatmon ran for a seat on the city commission. In 1963, Albany Movement President Slater King ran for mayor. A record 11,500 Albanians cast ballots in the three-man race. King came in second with over 2,500 votes losing to moderate segregationist James V. Davis.

secure the radio promotions, and distribute the posters announcing the rally. A.C. Searles, editor of the *Albany Southwest Georgian*, was the campaign director. King opened the campaign with an outdoor rally in Cuthbert in mid-April 1964, and the impact of the campaign on voter registration was immediate. One week in July saw the registration of over 1,200 African Americans in southwest Georgia, including over 40 (before whites ran the SNCC workers out of town) in Bainbridge, home of Maston Emmett O'Neal, Jr., who ultimately defeated King. C.B. King may have lost the election, but he proved that African Americans could not only vote, they could run for Congress.

The summer of C.B. King's congressional campaign also witnessed passage of the Civil Rights Act of 1964 which, among other things, outlawed discrimination in public accommodations. In mid-July, Albany Movement President Slater King called an end to the economic boycott, and the following spring public bus service in Albany was restored. Most businessmen in town

SNCC Executive Director James Forman with SNCC Field Secretary Ralph Allen as Allen is released from the Terrell County jail.
Danny Lyon/Magnum Photos

begrudgingly adhered to the new law and served black and white customers. People testing public accommodations the next winter were pleased with compliance; one civil rights leader said "compliance probably was greater in Albany than it was in Atlanta." In fall 1964, the Albany city commission authorized Chief Pritchett to hire six African American policemen. For some people in Albany the world was changing fast.

But not fast enough for African Americans. Whites who had oppressed them all their lives did not miraculously change their attitudes towards people of color. Jim Crow may have legally died, but it lived on in the hearts and minds of most white Albanians. For example, the black policemen whom Chief Pritchett hired could work only in African American neighborhoods. The Tift Park pool was still off limits to people of color. In July, SNCC worker Don Harris, one of the Americus Four, and nine others were arrested and convicted for trying to gain admission to the former city pool. And the Dougherty County school board resisted until the last minute a federal court order to integrate the senior class at Albany High School. School

integration at this time followed the "freedom of choice" model. Six brave African American young women—Joann Christian, Mamie Nell Ford, Shirley Lawrence, Eddie Maude McKendrick, Beverly Plummer, and Rubye Nell Singleton—volunteered to be the first students of color at Albany High School. Their senior year was a living hell. They were assigned to separate classes to isolate them further. In the cafeteria white students spat on them and refused to sit with them. So the six African Americans would sit at different tables, causing a white evacuation at each. Joann Christian recalled how Rev. Samuel Wells accompanied them to every football game and would "sit in the bleachers with us, bless his heart. While we watched the game, people threw liquor, firecrackers, sodas, everything—you name it—at us. Reverend Wells sat through it all with us. . . . We went to every game in town. Every game." The six girls persevered through the taunts of their white class-mates, including Paula Deen, and graduated on schedule.

The summer of their graduation—1965—saw a revival of the movement in Americus and the introduction of protest into that bastion of white supremacy, Bad Baker. The

Americus Movement generated national headlines with its five integration marches with more than 200 protestors each, accompanied by some violence, mostly whites beating protestors, and a Ku Klux Klan march drawing 700 Klan members and sympathizers. Sumter County appointed three black voting clerks and in two days 647 African Americans registered to vote. In the meantime, African Americans in Baker County began standing up to the feared Sheriff Gator Johnson. The event that "changed everything in Baker County," according to Shirley Miller Sherrod, was the March 15 murder of her father Hosie Miller by his white neighbor Cal Hall over the ownership of several cows. Miller was the gentle soul who posted Charlie Ware's bond in 1963; Hall shot him in the back when Miller suggested they take their dispute to court. The Baker County grand jury investigated and said there was not enough evidence to prosecute Hall for murder. By June, a small group of African Americans met, formed the Baker County Movement, and called on Charles Sherrod

School Board was violating its own "freedom of choice" integration plan by prohibiting qualified African American students from attending the white county schools. The federal office immediately investigated the situation and learned that 160 black parents had signed forms for their children to attend the white schools, yet the Baker County School Board approved only seven students to enter the white schools. When federal officials said that 85 black students should be allowed in the white schools, Baker County school board attorney B.C. Gardner countered that such a number would require "bring[ing] in Federal troops." In March 1966, the Office of Education finally took the first step to cut off federal funding for the Baker County schools.

In the meantime, the handful of black students who attended the white school suffered abuse similar to that of the first black students who had integrated Albany High School. At the beginning of the new year, 1966, night riders burned a black church in Baker County to register their

C.B. King may have lost the election, but he proved that African Americans could not only vote, they could run for Congress.

and SNCC for assistance. Sherrod organized a protest march at the courthouse in Newton on July 21. A group of whites attacked the marchers, pummeling Sherrod while Newton Police Chief James Holt looked on. When asked why no arrests for assault were made, Newton police officer Frank Jones said it was "just a fight between the civilians and the colored."

Fearful for their lives, a group of 30 African Americans, including Sherrod and Shirley Miller, slipped out of Baker County and drove to Washington, DC, to ask the Justice Department, the vice president, Congress, and other government officials to provide them protection in the form of an injunction when they returned to Baker County. They complained that their sheriff "called himself 'Gator Johnson' and made noises like an alligator to scare Negroes." What they wanted was to go home and register to vote and "send their children to integrated schools" without harassment.

While in Washington, Sherrod delivered to the Office of Education a SNCC complaint that the Baker County

unhappiness with the movement. Then in March 1966, white supremacists on the Baker County commission, fearful that 65-year-old African American Walter Singletary might win election as justice of the peace, cancelled the election shortly before it was to happen. They also abolished the justice of the peace post.

In 1966, it became clear that the freedom struggle in southwest Georgia was at another turning point. SNCC, which had been integral to the southwest Georgia movement since its arrival in 1961, was experiencing significant change on the national level as more and more African American members embraced Black Power. Sherrod, who believed in the importance of using white and black SNCC workers in the Southwest Georgia Project, found this new development troubling. As he struggled with how to handle Black Power, SNCC, and the Southwest Georgia Project, he married his life partner Shirley Miller in September 1966. Together the Sherrods would help shape the contours of the next half-century of the southwest Georgia freedom struggle.

The restored sanctuary of Old Mt. Zion Church looking south towards the pulpit. Todd Stone Photography

12

The freedom struggle continued in southwest Georgia for the rest of the 20th century in the areas of education, the economy, politics, and criminal justice. At the same time, civil rights leaders were at the forefront of remembering and celebrating the struggle from the first anniversary celebration of the Albany Movement in 1962 to the opening of a civil rights museum in the Old Mt. Zion sanctuary in 1998. And through the last three decades of the century, cases like the Dawson Five and Chicken Pie Six reminded people that the freedom struggle was not over in southwest Georgia.

Even before the first African American girls desegregated Albany High School in 1964, whites could read the hand-writing on the wall. A number of white leaders throughout the region, determined their children would be taught in all-

year before the Albany public schools, "under orders from the Bishop of Savannah." But it was the exception to the rule.

The rash of white academy openings in fall 1970 coincided with a 1969 federal court order that all Georgia public schools be desegregated by September 1970. Any school district not in compliance would lose its state funding (about 75 percent of local school districts' budgets). Most local districts implemented plans to move some black teachers to white schools and vice versa. Black students were moved to white schools but very few white students were assigned to black schools. The reluctance of white students to attend African American schools was also true at the collegiate level. White Albanians felt the need for a college in town in the 1960s, never considering

THE SOUTHWEST GEORGIA FREEDOM STRUGGLE
TO THE END OF THE 20TH CENTURY,
1967-2000

white schools, organized private academies. Among the first in southwest Georgia was the Deerfield School in Albany. Windsor Park Academy and Riverview Academy were also organized in Albany. Parents in rural counties soon followed suit with Randolph Southern School in Shellman (1966), Crisp Academy in Cordele (1967), Brookwood School in Thomasville (1970), Terrell Academy in Dawson (1970), Southwest Georgia Academy in Damascus (1970), Southland Academy in Americus (1970), Westwood School in Camilla (1971), and Worth Academy in Sylvester (1971). When Sumter County's Southland Academy opened, over 1,000 students enrolled leaving the public schools 80 percent black. Like many rural counties, Sumter reduced its property taxes and its funding for the majority black public schools. Not all private schools were founded to maintain segregation. St. Teresa's Catholic Church in Albany founded its parochial school in 1945 and integrated in 1963, one

the possibility of attending the local four-year school, Albany State College, because it was historically black. In 1963 they established Albany Junior College (AJC) and, in 1966, classes began on the 100-acre campus. Albany citizens purchased the land and paid for AJC's first five buildings. Like ASC, AJC was a unit of the University System of Georgia, and, several times in the ensuing decades, efforts were made to merge the two institutions. ASC supporters, aware of the fact that when a black and a white public school merged it usually meant the end of the black institution, forestalled the perennial merger talks and the two institutions—now Albany State University and Darton State College—flourish independently. Ironically, both schools now have majority black student populations.

As AJC students wrapped up their first fall quarter in December 1966, Black Power advocates in SNCC voted to expel its white members. When word reached the

The restored sanctuary of Old Mt. Zion Church looking north towards the entrance. From 1998 to 2010 the pews in the rear of the church were in storage and the open area served as the exhibit space for the Albany Civil Rights Movement Museum. Todd Stone Photography

newly-wed Sherrods, Charles, who had made black and white teams central to the Southwest Georgia Project, resigned noting, "I didn't leave the SNCC, the SNCC left me." The Sherrods then founded the Southwest Georgia Project for Community Education. As they strove to achieve economic equality in rural southwest Georgia, their vision for a communal black farming operation began to take shape.

In 1968, Slater King, Charles Sherrod, and four others went to Israel to study the kibbutz system of farming. There they observed moshavim, collective farms where individuals cultivated small plots on their own and worked communally on large fields, sharing the major costs such as machinery as well as apportioning the profits. The moshav became the model for New Communities, Inc. (NCI), the African American communal agricultural project that the Sherrods established in 1969. Their

ambitious goal was to become the first "self-sustaining black community land trust in America," with jobs for 300 and improvement in their education, health care, and housing by 1974. Slater King used his real estate connections to purchase the 4,800-acre "Featherfield Farm" in Lee County for the project.

From the start, NCI faced immense hurdles. The NCI board scrambled to come up with the more than $1 million cost of the property, eventually securing an $800,000 mortgage from the Prudential Insurance Company. But the lack of long-range financing and the shortage of laborers at crucial times (calls for volunteers did result in northern student help) plagued the Lee County cooperative. The enterprise also faced some old enemies, including night rider attacks, accusations of communism, and the hostility of local government officials who opposed NCI's efforts to get federal loans.

After three years, despite all its efforts, NCI had just 10 families, living in old houses, cultivating 1,000 acres. The following year, 1973, turned out to be its best year and NCI made a net profit of nearly $150,000. Still, contributions were necessary to meet the enormous mortgage payments and operating expenses each year. Then, in August 1974, the United Farm Workers led 50 of NCI's farm laborers, most of them under age 16, out on strike complaining of low wages and inhumane working conditions. A month later, management and eight workers were the only ones harvesting the crops. NCI survived its labor troubles, and, like many farmers, turned to the federal government for assistance in the form of loans. But federal Farm Home Administration (FHA) loans had to be approved by the local FHA administrator who assured Sherrod that any such loan to NCI would be "over my dead body." Even when federal authorities compelled the local officials to approve the loans, it was usually too little,

Nation of Islam purchased a 1,800-acre farm in Terrell County on which they raised cattle, wheat and vegetables "to provide a food supply for Black Muslims . . . elsewhere." Shortly after the Sherrods bought the Lee County land for NCI, the Nation of Islam (NOI) acquired an additional 2,200 acres expanding its Terrell County farm to 4,000 acres. "Mismanagement, poor leadership, and foundering hopes," however, characterized the Black Muslim farm in the 1970s and early 1980s. In 1983, only 14 African American families lived in mobile homes on the place. The farm's unofficial caretaker at the time, Earl Ali Pasha, felt that the lack of farming experience was their biggest obstacle to success. Elijah Muhammad's son and successor W. Deen Muhammad eventually sold the Terrell County operation. Louis Farrakhan, the leader of a new NOI faction, bought 1,556 acres of the former NOI property in 1994 and NOI continued to operate it as Muhammad Farms well into the new century.

In December 1966, Black Power advocates in SNCC voted to expel its white members. When word reached the newly-wed Sherrods, Charles, who had made black and white teams central to the Southwest Georgia Project, resigned noting, "I didn't leave the SNCC, the SNCC left me."

too late. When a five-year drought began in 1979, white farmers were able to survive by building small irrigation systems with federal emergency loan money. But when NCI requested such a loan, it was denied. The combination of Mother Nature and an intransigent federal government brought on NCI's collapse in 1985. After 16 years of struggle to make his dream for an African American landowning farm community a reality, the determined Sherrod refused to give up. Eventually, he and Shirley and other black farmers joined a class action suit against the U.S. Department of Agriculture for its discriminatory practices towards African American farmers. Their patience eventually paid off but they would have to wait until the new millennium.

New Communities, Inc. was not the only, nor even the earliest, experiment in communal black landownership in southwest Georgia. In 1966, Elijah Muhammad's

African American concerns for economic equality extended beyond the rural counties of southwest Georgia to the region's urban centers, especially Albany. A decade after Martin Luther King's participation in the Albany Movement, the city of Albany continued its longtime discrimination against African American employees. Black city workers held the lowest paid blue collar jobs, endured segregated employee facilities from restrooms to coffee pots, and attended segregated Christmas parties and other employee functions. In fall 1971, Albany public works department employee Johnnie Johnson and a water department worker contacted the Laborers International Union of North America about organizing the city's employees. The following spring, the city commission denied Laborer's Local 1309's request "for recognition and collective bargaining." Shortly afterwards, Johnnie Johnson got in an argument with his boss and was fired,

Shiloh Baptist Church and Mt. Zion Baptist Church, across the street from each other, were ground zero for the Albany Movement.
Todd Stone Photography

triggering a strike by 260 black city workers. Using direct action tactics African Americans had employed 10 years earlier, the strikers picketed city buildings and threatened to boycott black merchants who did not support them. The city ordered its striking employees back to work or lose their jobs. Eventually the strike ended and the city rehired a little over a third of the fired workers.

In summer 1972, Johnnie Johnson and five other city employees turned to attorney C.B. King and his partner Herbert E. Phipps for legal help, and, in August, they filed a class action suit against the city for racial discrimination. Following years of extensive discovery, Federal District Judge Wilbur Owens finally heard the case in March 1976. Two months later, he ruled against the city arguing that although segregation had ended and discrimination had lessened, "it nevertheless continues to the present day." Owens issued a permanent injunction requiring the city to increase its

commission seats diluted black votes, preventing those areas of the city and county with majority black populations from electing black commissioners.

Once again, African Americans turned to Wilbur Owens's federal district court for relief. Fanny Paige and three other African Americans, representing all black citizens of Albany, sued the city in 1975. Leading the legal team was African American attorney Mary Moss Young, who had earned her civil rights stripes as a student activist in Fitzgerald, Georgia. She persuaded Judge Owens with strong evidence that the 1947 state law changing Albany's ward system of elections to at-large voting resulted in diluting the majority black vote in certain wards. Owens determined the 1947 at-large voting act to be unconstitutional and issued a permanent injunction on August 16, 1975 changing Albany city elections back to ward voting for the November 4 election. He redrew the old boundaries of

Black city workers [in Albany] held the lowest paid blue collar jobs, endured segregated employee facilities from restrooms to coffee pots, and attended segregated Christmas parties and other employee functions.

African American employment through the use of racial quotas in hiring and promotion. Half of those hired and promoted were to be African American. Judge Owens was determined to eliminate discrimination in Albany. While hearing a case in 1976, he learned that the desegregated bathrooms in the courthouse were locked and that only white employees had keys. He told the city to go right then to remove the locks to the courthouse restrooms. Judge Owens lifted his injunction 19 years later, officially ending the use of racial quotas in the city's affirmative action plan in 1995.

The Johnnie Johnson case illustrated what happens when the political leadership of a multiracial community remained lily white. White leaders had no incentive to hire black employees until the federal courts intervened and forced them to do so. Only with the election of African American leaders would change be effected; but the local political system in Albany and southwest Georgia was designed to prevent the election of black officials. At-large voting for the city and county

the city's five wards, two of which had a black majority. When voters went to the polls in Wards 2 and 3 on November 4, they elected African Americans—Mary Young and Robert Montgomery—the first blacks ever elected to the Albany city commission. The following year, the Criterion Club of Albany filed a class-action suit against the Dougherty County commission to change its county at-large elections to district elections. Before the case could be heard, the parties settled and the state legislature provided for district elections in Dougherty. In fall 1978, the first two African Americans—James Bush and Don Cutler—were elected to the county commission.

The first African American elected to represent Dougherty County in the Georgia House of Representatives since Ishmael Lonon's term in 1880-1881 was John White, WALB-TV's first black newscaster, in 1974. In 1976, Charles Sherrod was elected to the Albany city commission where he served for 14 years. More amazing, that same year, his mother-in-law, Grace Miller, was elected to the Baker County School Board, a seat she would hold for more than three decades. At the same Baker County election, voters elected Scroot Johnson, Gator's son, to succeed his father as sheriff. Scroot was arrested by federal authorities in 1982 for embezzlement and tax evasion and he did some time in prison. Scroot's brother, Herbert, lost election as sheriff thus ending the Johnson family's control of that office. In 1996, Baker County voters elected their first African American sheriff, Isaac Anderson. Meanwhile in Terrell County, Dawson voters in 1991 elected their first African American mayor, undertaker Robert Albritten.

These African American electoral successes, however, were not universal and many rural counties maintained at-large systems for electing county commissions. In 1977, the American Civil Liberties Union filed suit against Sumter and Terrell counties, neither of which had had any black elected officials. The year before, African American Ernest Johnson lost his bid for a seat on the Dawson city

several of them. They were charged with the capital offense of first degree murder and languished in the Terrell County jail for between nine and nineteen months before they were released on bail provided by attorney Millard Farmer's Team Defense Project and Morris Dees's Southern Poverty Law Center. Part of Farmer's legal strategy was to put Dawson on trial, expose its sickening racism, and show how the Dawson Five were "prisoners of a system . . . prisoners of a closed society, a society which wants to perpetuate white supremacy . . . white control over the black person." The first half of August 1977 was devoted to pretrial hearings during which Farmer tried to get the indictments dismissed. Judge W.I. Geer, however, rejected the charges of police misconduct and ordered the first of separate trials for each of the five to begin at the end of August.

There followed a series of delays and the trials were rescheduled to start on December 27, 1977. Then in mid-December, Judge Geer suppressed the disputed confession

While hearing a case in 1976, [Judge Wilbur Owens] learned that the desegregated bathrooms in the courthouse were locked and that only white employees had keys. He told the city to go right then to remove the locks to the courthouse restrooms.

council. On Election Day, whites manning the polls were unable to find the names of 70 African Americans whom Johnson had personally taken to register to vote. According to Sardis Baptist Church pastor Rev. M.W. Merritt, African Americans in Terrell County were "a hopeless, fear-ridden people because of the brutalities that have been perpetrated in this country by white people historically." That was an apt description of the five young Terrell County men in their late teens and early 20s who became known to the world as the Dawson Five.

Their story began in January 1976 with a holdup and murder at a Dawson crossroads convenience store and evolved into a major civil rights case. Once again, national and international media attention was riveted on race in Terrible Terrell. Although the five semiliterate African Americans denied being anywhere near the store at the time of the murder, Dawson police used the threat of castration, electrocution, and a cocked pistol between the eyes of one of the youths to coerce confessions out of

of Roosevelt Watson, the first of the Dawson Five to be tried. With no tangible evidence (the murder weapon was never found) and no allowable confession, the prosecution moved to dismiss the case against the Dawson Five. Three of the five black youths left town, one of them saying, "Dawson is no place for a Black man." Earlier that summer, another young African American in Dawson, Usher Bridges, observed the seemingly unchanged racial picture of Terrible Terrell: "That's how the white people are; they're going to be by themselves. They've got the power, the money. When it's over, we're still got to be catching hell."

One of the bright spots in southwest Georgia race relations was at Sumter County's interracial community at Koinonia, a frequent meeting place for civil rights workers in the 1960s. Several important projects had their birth at Koinonia before breaking away as separate entities. The most notable example was the world famous Habitat for Humanity. Less well-known and more short-lived was the Prison and Jail Project (PJP) which played an important role in the region's freedom struggle near the end of the 20th century. Led by John Cole Vodicka and headquartered in Americus, the PJP attacked racial discrimination in the region's criminal justice system between 1993 and 2008. Its tiny staff advocated on behalf of prisoners and their families, visited the jails of southwest Georgia, observed courtroom proceedings and reported on them in their regular publication, *Freedomways*.

Each fall, the PJP conducted a weeklong 80- to 100-mile Freedom Walk along the roads and highways of rural southwest Georgia, calling attention to the racism and abuse that riddled the region's courts and jails. The 1998 Freedom Walk culminated at the Mitchell County Courthouse in Camilla on September 19, the 130th anniversary of the Camilla Massacre, and publicly observed that occasion for the first time in the city's history. When the 1999 Freedom Walk entered Smithville

as full-time chief judge of the Dougherty County Magistrate Court. In 1999, Judge Phipps was appointed to the Court of Appeals of Georgia, and, in 2013, became chief judge of that court. President Bill Clinton's appointment of W. Louis Sands as the first African American judge of the federal district court for the Middle District of Georgia was confirmed by the U.S. Senate in 1994. In Dougherty County, appointed leadership positions were eventually filled by African Americans, including Albany Police Chief Washington Long (1988), Albany Fire Chief Henry L. Fields (1991) and Dougherty County School Superintendent John Culbreath (1995).

Remembering and celebrating past achievements has always been an important part of movement culture. In November 1962, the Albany Movement began a tradition of observing the anniversary of the movement's founding on November 17, 1961. Dr. King returned to Albany and spoke at a mass meeting at Third Kiokee Baptist Church

Part of Farmer's legal strategy was to put Dawson on trial, expose its sickening racism, and show how the Dawson Five were "prisoners of a system . . . prisoners of a closed society, a society which wants to perpetuate white supremacy."

in northern Lee County, the police chief issued citations to six Freedom Walkers who became known as the Chicken Pie Six (after Smithville's annual Chicken Pie Festival). The Chicken Pie Six stood trial in November for violating Smithville's parade permit ordinance, but the charges were dropped when the judge determined the city law to be an unconstitutional infringement on free speech.

The 1990s saw an important expansion in African American political, judicial, and administrative leadership. For the first time in the region's history, southwest Georgians elected a black congressman in 1992. Sanford Bishop of Columbus won the second congressional district seat that C.B. King had contested three decades earlier and successfully held on to his seat well into the new millennium. African Americans also made inroads in the local, state, and federal judiciary. In 1980, Herbert E. Phipps became the first black magistrate and associate judge of the Dougherty County State Court. In 1993, Willie E. Lockette was the first African American to serve

as part of the weeklong celebration. In 1991, Mayor Tommy Coleman established the Albany Movement Historical Commission to commemorate the history of the movement. Early on, the commission realized the need to establish a museum to remember and honor the Albany Movement. Commissioners McCree Harris, Bee McCormack, and Lee Formwalt approached the Mt. Zion Baptist Church deacon board about acquiring the old dilapidated sanctuary, no longer used by the church, for a civil rights museum. The city's and county's political leaders agreed to allocate $1 million to renovate the Old Mt. Zion Church into the Albany Civil Rights Movement Museum, which opened in 1998. Ten years later, an additional $4 million from the city expanded the museum into the much larger and technologically sophisticated Albany Civil Rights Institute. And supporting all of these efforts was the *Albany Herald* and WALB-TV, which in the early 1960s had campaigned vigorously against King and the black struggle to destroy Jim Crow.

In 2014, Shiloh Baptist Church continued to be led by Rev. H.C. Boyd, who first opened the church to the movement in 1961.
Todd Stone Photography

13

The southwest Georgia freedom struggle continued in the new millennium and was marked by political achievements along with some setbacks. The Sherrods continued their leadership role and witnessed the rebirth of New Communities, Inc. The Southwest Georgia Project for Community Education continued to make a difference. Meanwhile, downtown Albany was the site of revitalization efforts, several of which were directly related to the region's African American heritage. Educational successes were accompanied by disappointments as the region's high rate of poverty stubbornly resisted change.

As southwest Georgians entered the 21st century, many of them continued to live in majority black counties. In fact, over one-half of the 25 Georgia counties with a 50 percent or higher African American population were in

1990, Dougherty's African Americans comprised one-half, and by 2000, two-thirds of the county's population. These population trends would continue for the most part into the new millennium and would affect not only education, but politics, race relations, the economy and the persistence of poverty in southwest Georgia.

As a result of local African American efforts and outside intervention by organizations like the American Civil Liberties Union, which used the 1965 Voting Rights Act and its subsequent modifications to take to federal court many southwest Georgia city and county commissions, at-large voting was replaced by single district voting in much of southwest Georgia. At the same time, African American voter registration continued to increase. In counties like Lee, Baker, and Terrell, with less than 2.5

21ST-CENTURY SOUTHWEST GEORGIA,
2001-2014

the southwest region of the state. The two counties in southwest Georgia to see the most significant population change in terms of race were Lee and Dougherty. These adjacent counties both began the 20th century over 80 percent black. By 1950, among Dougherty's nearly 44,000 people, whites outnumbered blacks for the first time in the county's history; whereas in Lee, African Americans comprised nearly three-quarters of its shrinking population of less than 7,000. Both counties experienced population growth of in-migrating whites at the expense of out-migrating blacks in the 1960s. That trend would continue in Lee County for the rest of the 20th century so that by 2000, the former black majority county had more than tripled its population, but only 16 percent of it was African American. Lee County had become Dougherty's white bedroom community due to the latter county's white exodus. Dougherty's white flight began in the 1970s with the integration of its public schools. By

percent of their eligible black populations registered to vote in 1962, the change over the next four decades was seismic. In 2004, registered African Americans in those three counties comprised between two-thirds and three-quarters of their eligible black populations. These changes led to an increase in the number of black elected officials throughout the region. For the first time, in 2004, Albany voters elected an African American mayor, obstetrician Willie Adams. Dr. Adams defeated the longtime white incumbent Tommy Coleman with 60 percent of the vote and won reelection in 2007. In the 2011 mayoral race, John White, Albany's first black representative in the Georgia Assembly in the 20th century, placed third, leaving the runoff to two women, black former city commissioner Dorothy Hubbard and white businesswoman B.J. Fletcher. Hubbard won the close race, becoming the first woman and second African American to win election as Albany mayor.

The century-old Bartow Powell House, on the same block as ACRI and Shiloh Baptist Church, was lovingly restored by charismatic businessman and political activist Hank Young. *Todd Stone Photography*

The year Dr. Willie Adams won reelection as Albany mayor—2007—the citizens of Camilla elected their first African American and first female mayor, Mary Jo Haywood. Working with a majority white male city council, unenthusiastic about changing the status quo, was a challenge; in her last year in office, the council voted 5-1 to censure the mayor for her management style. The one commissioner who voted against censure, Vivian Smith, in a telling comment said, "I think we're acting like children." Mayor Haywood responded to the censure resolution, which she viewed as "clearly intended to tie my hands or limit my ability to serve." She told the councilors she had no intention of resigning and reminded them that the people—not the council—had hired her and she would continue to serve them the rest of her term. Six months later, on September 19, 2011, the mayor called for a "moment of silence" to "honor the memory of those who died in the Camilla Massacre" 143 years earlier. The mayor hoped that in the next year a healing ceremony would "bring descendants of both sides together. Then, perhaps, the descendants of the attackers can ask for forgiveness on behalf of their ancestors and the descendants of the killed can accept that forgiveness on behalf of their ancestors." The mayor concluded her Camilla Massacre observance announcement by noting that "One of those killed that day was an 'Unknown Freed Woman' who has served as an inspiration to me. I feel that each time a woman stands up for right that 'unknown' lady takes a name. She and the others did not die in vain! For her, especially, and for each of them I am honored today to sign this as, *Mayor Mary Jo Haywood.*"

Mayor Haywood's term expired at the beginning of 2012. That year, another black mayor, mortician Robert Albritten, the 21-year incumbent mayor of Dawson, faced a challenge from Christopher Wright, a 22-year-old African American student at Albany Technical Institute. Dawson citizens had grown tired of their longtime mayor, who had several run-ins with the law over the years, including DUI charges in 2003 and 2007 and a 12-month probation and $9,000 fine for falsifying life insurance forms in 2005. On Election Day, in a stunning upset, Dawson voters threw out the incumbent and took a chance on the young wet-behind-the-ears tech student, who also worked as an associate in County Commissioner Ernest Johnson's funeral home, along with funeral director and County Commissioner Lucius Holloway. A mature churchgoing young adult, Wright realized he had to deal with "the overall mistrust people have of leadership" in Dawson. In a newspaper interview less than three months after his election, Wright said, "I truly believe to make things better, we're going to have to fix ourselves from the inside out." When asked about the challenges he had to face, he impishly grinned, "One of

words that would resonate with many African Americans, he said the GBI officers "interrogate me as if I brought this on myself. They implied maybe I was involved in illegal drugs or some sort of love triangle. I thought that was a bit absurd."

The same year Dawson citizens elected their youngest ever mayor, Democratic primary voters in Baker County went to their five polls scattered around the rural county to select a new member of the county commission to represent the overwhelmingly black Hoggard Mill district. Unfortunately, for 62-year-old African American candidate Emmett Miller, Baker was one of those southwest Georgia counties that still held at-large elections for its all-white county commission. Kevin Coker, his white opponent, defeated him on July 31, 2012. Miller felt he had a good chance of winning since he thought Baker's population was majority black. Blacks had had a slight majority as recently as 2000. In the new century, however, both blacks and whites had

On Election Day, in a stunning upset, Dawson voters threw out the incumbent [mayor] and took a chance on the young wet-behind-the-ears tech student.

the things that I've learned since I've been in office is how to cuss," he said. "Now I know my mom and dad are not going to like reading that, but as stupid as it sounds, that's sometimes the only way you can get things done around here."

Like Mary Jo Haywood, Christopher Wright shook up the political establishment. And like her, he faced resistance. Some argue that that resistance took a violent turn on Halloween night 2013. When the 23-year-old mayor returned to his home late that night, two masked men lying in wait shot him six times. Hospitalized in critical condition, he was released after 24 days. In the meantime, the Dawson city council voted 4-2 to deny him a 24-hour guard until his attackers could be arrested. In a TV news interview in January 2014, the recovering mayor said, "I do live in fear. I do. The assailants haven't been caught, and I have no idea who this was." Then in

left Baker County; but more blacks than whites departed, leaving a slight white majority, enough to insure Coker's victory. Even Coker felt the at-large system in Baker County was unfair: "Our county is messed up. I think they need black representation on our county commission. I think that would cost me my job, but right is right and wrong is wrong." But, apparently not wrong enough to compel Coker to withdraw from his campaign for the county commission seat.

The new, still all-white Baker County commission considered a cost-cutting measure at the end of 2013 that would be another setback for African Americans if enacted. The plan, proposed by the county board of elections, was to eliminate four of the county's polling places, including the one in the Hoggard Mill precinct, leaving only one in Newton. Before the U.S. Supreme Court suspended Section 5 of the Voting Rights Act in

The Albany Civil Rights Movement Museum was transformed into the Albany Civil Rights Institute with the opening of new exhibit space in 2008. Todd Stone Photography

2013, such a change would be subject to Department of Justice review. That was no longer the case. In October 2013, the NAACP beseeched the county to reconsider going ahead with the poll elimination plan. Initially, Coker was skeptical of the proposal, but by December 2013, he supported it. If he were black, however, he said he might "have a different perspective and oppose it."

Baker County native Shirley Sherrod and her husband Charles continued their leading role in the southwest Georgia freedom struggle after 2000. Earlier, they had filed a claim in the black farmers' class action suit, *Pigford v. Glickman* (1999), seeking compensation from the U.S. Department of Agriculture for discrimination against New Communities, Inc. (NCI) in the 1980s. In July 2009, they learned that their claim had been approved and that NCI would be awarded $12 million and that Shirley and Charles would each get an additional $150,000 for the "mental anguish" they had

endured. Two years later, the Sherrods, after consulting with the NCI families, used the *Pigford* settlement money to purchase Cypress Pond Plantation, a 1,638-acre estate southwest of Albany. The Paul E. Tarver Estate bought Cypress Pond for Paul's widow, Cinderella Tarver, and her 30-45 enslaved workers in 1860. At the start of the Civil War, she married Dr. Charles P. Heartwell who was the first Dougherty County planter to sell farmland to a former slave. It seemed appropriate that this plantation with its historical connection to local black landowning should become the new home for New Communities. In 2013, NCI finalized a master plan to use the plantation as a conference center and a farm for "racial healing and economic opportunity for farmers." Renamed Resora Plantation, it was opened to the public in June 2014.

In 2011, around the time that NCI acquired Cypress Pond, the Southwest Georgia Project for Community

Education hosted in June the first of two major golden anniversary celebrations of the Albany and Southwest Georgia Movement. Returning to Albany for the event was a number of former SNCC workers as well as Dr. Anderson. In addition to reflecting on the past, the Southwest Georgia Project continued to address current racial issues. In spring 2013, the project's racial healing coordinator, Harriet Hollis, got involved in Wilcox County's first ever integrated prom. The prom, like all proms held since Wilcox County High School was integrated in 1970, was unofficial and off school grounds. What made this prom in 2013 different was that it was not segregated. The tensions in the community were palpable as the prom organizers prepared to break a 40-year-old tradition of segregated spring dances. The event generated a media stir; some friends stopped talking to each other over the matter. Hollis knew that

music, left Albany with his mother a few months after his birth; but Albany still claims him as a native son. A block north of the plaza is the restored Bridge House built in 1858 by celebrated African American bridge builder Horace King at the west end of the first Flint River bridge in Albany. A quick glance at the metal historical marker hints at how far the city has come since the days of Jim Crow. The permanent sign, erected before the 1960s civil rights movement, refers to King by his first name only. Today, the Albany Welcome Center touts the importance of Horace King's contribution to building Albany's mid-19th-century infrastructure.

The third revitalization project honoring southwest Georgia African Americans is the new 12,315-square-foot expansion of ACRI built to house the museum's exhibit space. Once the old exhibits were removed from the rear half of the Old Mt. Zion Church (the front half of the

The tensions in the community were palpable as the prom organizers prepared to break a 40-year-old tradition of segregated spring dances.

pulling off such a controversial event was a delicate affair. "Talking about race in a small town," she said, "is a quick way to risk everything." Some of the students were willing to take that risk, and 100 people attended the integrated prom held in nearby Cordele. Among the curious onlookers and well-wishers was Shirley Sherrod. Several weeks later, Wilcox County High School announced that the school would officially host the 2014 prom for the first time since 1970.

The first decade of the 21st century witnessed a significant downtown revitalization program in Albany that included three projects honoring African Americans in the city's past. In 2007-2008, the city opened Ray Charles Plaza, the Albany Welcome Center in the restored Bridge House, and a major expansion of the Albany Civil Rights Museum rechristened the Albany Civil Rights Institute (ACRI). A life-size statue of Albany native Ray Charles (1930-2004) seated at and playing a piano dominates the plaza overlooking the Flint River. Charles, who won worldwide acclaim as a pioneer of soul

church was restored in 1998 to the way the church looked in 1961), the pews from the original back half of the church were restored and placed in the former exhibition space. Today, the church sanctuary is fully restored to the way it looked at the beginning of the Albany Movement. In late 2009, ACRI began offering public programming which interpreted the southwest Georgia freedom struggle as a two-century movement. Visitors to ACRI are reminded that hundreds of African American men voted in the 1860s and 1870s and that African Americans died in places like Camilla defending their constitutional rights of free speech and assembly. Thus, the civil rights movement of the 1960s was not about getting the vote, but getting the vote *back*— getting in the 1960s the rights their ancestors exercised with federal protection in the 1860s.

The culmination of ACRI's public programming in 2011 was the second observance of the Albany Movement's golden anniversary that year. Former SNCC workers returned again to Albany as did Dr. Anderson

The "Before 1961" section of the ACRI permanent exhibit features an interactive juke box that plays white and black tunes from the 1950s.
Todd Stone Photography

who spoke in Old Mt. Zion Baptist Church on November 17—50 years to the day that the Albany Movement was formally organized. The last and perhaps most powerful of the 50th anniversary events was the reunion of many of the ASC students expelled or suspended for civil rights activities in late 1961. They attended ASU's fall commencement in December at which ASU President Everette Freeman presented each of them with an honorary baccalaureate degree.

As the southwest Georgia freedom struggle concludes its second century, it is clear that in very important ways significant victories have been won. The cruel oppressive system of slavery was eliminated at great cost by 1865, and with federal protection, African American men in southwest Georgia exercised their franchise and, in Dougherty County, elected black men to represent them in the state legislature as late as 1880. They risked their

lives to vote until the power of white supremacy and the threat of lynching overwhelmed them in the early Jim Crow era of the late 19th and early 20th centuries. As the chains of sharecropping and crop lien replaced the chains of slavery, they continued to resist. Some, like a number of their slave ancestors who ran away, simply left southwest Georgia for the "Promised Land" up north. Others organized local branches of the NAACP and divisions of Marcus Garvey's UNIA. A few with luck and hard work became wealthy professionals and/or landowners. Like their enslaved forebears, they struggled and survived. They demanded more than elementary schools. When black high schools opened they filled the classrooms. Some went to college and some served their country in two world wars. After risking their lives for freedom overseas, they returned home only to experience the loss of freedom in Jim Crow Georgia. They organized, they sought allies in the federal government and elsewhere, they marched and they went to jail and they brought down Jim Crow. Progress was uneven and too slow, especially in the rural counties, but places like Terrible Terrell and Bad Baker eventually saw black voters electing African American mayors, commissioners, school board members and sheriffs. Public accommodations and schools were desegregated. Southwest Georgia in 2014 was a far different world from what it had been in 1864, 1914, or 1964.

But the freedom struggle in southwest Georgia is far from over. Racism and poverty work hand in hand to oppress many southwest Georgians of color. Everyone in the region feels the effects. Take, for example, segregated education. Segregation of public schools in most southwest Georgia counties ended in 1970. In the rural counties, like Terrell and Randolph, desegregation was momentary, replaced immediately by resegregation as whites fled the public schools to the newly created private academies. For a

The link between race and poverty is manifest in southwest Georgia. Racial discrimination in the region's unofficially segregated schools means there is less chance for poor African Americans to secure the education and skills needed to succeed economically. In 2009, Forbes.com named Albany one of the 10 poorest cities in the nation. Albany comprises much of Dougherty County which ranks 71st among Georgia's 159 counties in per capita income. Immediately to the north lies Lee County (with its 74 percent white population), which ranks 25th in per capita wealth. West of Lee is Terrell County (with its 61 percent black population) which ranks 141st in per capita wealth. The demography illustrates the segregation of poverty—Lee is rich and white and Terrell is poor and black. Another example of the segregation of poverty can be found within Dougherty County where the Flint River divides east Albany from the rest of the city. Black poverty is

In the rural counties, like Terrell and Randolph, desegregation was momentary, replaced immediately by resegregation as whites fled the public schools to the newly created private academies.

number of southwest Georgia counties, a dual school system prevails with black public schools and white private academies. In several of the rural counties, the percentages by race of the public and private student bodies almost mirror each other. For example, the percentage of black students in the Clay, Randolph, and Terrell public schools range from 92 to 94 percent, while the percentage of white students in those counties' private academies range from 98 to 99 percent. In Dougherty County, where the population is 67 percent African American, white flight has resulted in a public school system that is 80 percent black. In this somewhat cosmopolitan urban center of southwest Georgia, the leading college prep school is 88 percent white. Meanwhile, across the county line in Lee County, with its 74 percent white population, the public school population is 19 percent black. In a racially conscious society like southwest Georgia's, it is likely that Dougherty will grow blacker as more whites flee to Lee and its "better," i.e., whiter, schools.

concentrated in east and south Albany. East Albany is 90 percent African American and in 2010, its median household income ($19,601) was a little over one-half of that ($33,655) for the Albany Metropolitan Statistical Area (MSA). The unemployment rate in east Albany (18.6 percent) is more than double that of the Albany MSA (8.4 percent).

We have much to be proud of as we look back and see where we have come from since 1814. Political achievements in southwest Georgia have been substantial. We have been less successful in dealing with the racism of poverty. Or, as Charles Sherrod put it, "So, politically, we're on the ball, but we're still broke. Boss is still boss." It has become clear that political power is one thing, but real power in the 21st century is economic power. As we begin the third century of the southwest Georgia freedom struggle, it is in that direction that we need to head, inspired by the courage and spirit of those heroes in whose footsteps we dare to tread.

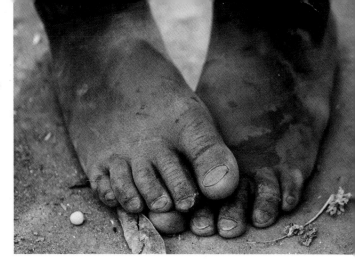

For Further Reading

ANTEBELLUM, CIVIL WAR, AND RECONSTRUCTION ERAS, 1814-1880

- Lee W. Formwalt, "Moving in 'That Strange Land of Shadows': African-American Mobility and Persistence in Post-Civil War Southwest Georgia," *Georgia Historical Quarterly* 82 (Fall 1998): 507–532.
- Lee W. Formwalt, ed., "Petitioning Congress for Protection: A Black View of Reconstruction at the Local Level," *Georgia Historical Quarterly* 73 (1989): 305-322.
- Susan Eva O'Donovan, *Becoming Free in the Cotton South* (Harvard University Press, 2007).
- David Williams, *Rich Man's War: Class, Caste, and Confederate Defeat in the Lower Chattahoochee Valley* (University of Georgia Press, 1998).

JIM CROW ERA, 1880-1959

- Aaron Brown, *The Negro in Albany* (1945).
- W.E.B. Du Bois, *The Souls of Black Folk* (Bedford Books, 1997/1903).
- Leon F. Litwack, *Trouble in Mind: Black Southerners in the Age of Jim Crow* (Alfred A. Knopf, Inc., 1998).
- Hugh Pearson, *Under the Knife: How a Wealthy Negro Surgeon Wielded Power in the Jim Crow South* (The Free Press, 2000).
- Mary G. Rolinson, *Grassroots Garveyism: The Universal Negro Improvement Association in the Rural South, 1920-1927* (University of North Carolina Press, 2007).
- Stephen G. N. Tuck, *Beyond Atlanta: The Struggle for Racial Equality in Georgia, 1940-1980* (University of Georgia Press, 2001).

ALBANY AND SOUTHWEST GEORGIA MOVEMENT, 1959-2014

- Raymond Arsenault, *Freedom Riders: 1961 and the Struggle for Racial Justice* (Oxford University Press, 2006).
- Taylor Branch, *Parting the Waters: America in the King Years 1954-63* (Simon and Schuster, 1988).
- Guy and Candie Carawan, *Sing for Freedom: The Story of the Civil Rights Movement Through Its Songs* (New South Books, 2007/1992).
- David L. Chappell, *Inside Agitators: White Southerners in the Civil Rights Movement* (Johns Hopkins University Press, 1994).
- Peter de Lissovoy, ed., *The Great Pool Jump & Other Stories from the Civil Rights Movement in Southwest Georgia* (YouArePerfectPress, 2010).
- David J. Garrow, *Bearing the Cross: Martin Luther King, Jr., and the Southern Christian Leadership Conference* (William Morrow and Company, 1986).
- Cheryl Lynn Greenberg, ed., *A Circle of Trust: Remembering SNCC* (Rutgers University Press, 1998).
- Faith S. Holsaert et al., eds., *Hands on the Freedom Plow: Personal Accounts by Women in SNCC* (University of Illinois Press, 2010).
- Danny Lyon, *Memories of the Southern Civil Rights Movement* (Twin Palms Publishers, 2010/1992).
- John Perdew, *Education of a Harvard Guy: Footsoldier in the Civil Rights Movement* (GrantHouse Publishers, 2010).
- Shirley Sherrod with Catherine Whitney, *The Courage to Hope: How I Stood Up to the Politics of Fear* (Atria Books, 2012).
- Sharon Thomason, *Raising Cane: A History of Bobs Candies, Inc.* (WH Wolfe Associates, 1990).
- Stephen G. N. Tuck, *Beyond Atlanta: The Struggle for Racial Equality in Georgia, 1940-1980* (University of Georgia Press, 2001).
- *Voices of the Civil Rights Movement: Black American Freedom Songs, 1960-1966* (Smithsonian Folkways Recordings, 1997), 2 CDs.
- Pat Watters, *Down to Now: Reflections on the Southern Civil Rights Movement* (University of Georgia Press, 1993/1971).
- Andrew Young, *An Easy Burden: The Civil Rights Movement and the Transformation of America* (HarperCollins, 1996).
- Howard Zinn, *The Southern Mystique* (South End Press, 2002).